5-INGREDIENT
CLEAN EATING
COOKBOOK

5-INGREDIENT
CLEAN EATING
COOKBOOK

125 Simple Recipes
to Nourish and Inspire

◇◇◇◇◇◇◇◇◇◇◇

Snezana Paucinac

Photography by Darren Muir

ROCKRIDGE
PRESS

TO MY MIA AND LUKA.
YOUR HAPPINESS IS MY
BIGGEST JOY IN LIFE.
AND TO MY HUSBAND,
DORIS, MY ROCK.
I LOVE THE LIFE WE
HAVE BUILT TOGETHER.

CONTENTS

INTRODUCTION • VIII

CHAPTER ONE

Eating Clean
Every Day • 1

CHAPTER TWO

Breakfasts • 17

CHAPTER THREE

Soups, Salads,
and Dressings • 35

CHAPTER FOUR

Snacks and
Small Plates • 55

CHAPTER FIVE

Rice, Grains, and Beans • 75

CHAPTER SIX

Plant-Based Meals • 99

CHAPTER SEVEN

Poultry and Meat • 123

CHAPTER EIGHT

Fish and Seafood • 137

CHAPTER NINE

Dressings, Sauces,
and Marinades • 153

CHAPTER TEN

Beverages and Desserts • 165

Index • 178

INTRODUCTION

My life growing up in southeastern Europe is something I look back to often. Most of the food we ate was farm-to-table and most meals were home cooked. We only ate out one or two times a year, if that. We spent our summers and winters in our village house high up in the mountains, where everybody ate only what grew in their yards. Milk was from the cows we took care of, and the meat we ate was wild, caught in the woods.

Fast-forward to the year 2000, when I moved to the United States with my mom. I was 19 years old in a foreign country where everything was super-sized, eating out was the norm, and everyone drove everywhere because walking around was a burden.

I gained more than 10 pounds in my first six months of living in the United States. My drink of choice was a Diet Coke, and although my mom cooked, I loved fast-food restaurants and would visit them frequently. After I started dating my childhood friend—who today is my husband—Boris (who also moved to the United States as a teenager), I started cooking more, but my diet was still very unhealthy. I enjoyed white-flour bagels daily, sandwiches with processed cold cuts at lunch, and endless bowls of home-cooked spaghetti and meatballs at night.

Within a few years, I had two beautiful kids, Mia and Luka. I ate healthy in both of my pregnancies (because books said I should), and I made my own baby food (again, books). It wasn't until my son turned eight months old that my cards started reshuffling. I was exercising more and more (weight training was a big part of my life then, and still is) and I started reading about workouts and about what exactly I was supposed to be eating. The more attention I paid to nutrition, the more benefits I saw, and the more I was intrigued by it. I soon realized that there is a big connection between clean eating and the way I feel. Right around the beginning of my transformation, my husband also started his journey of losing more than 50 pounds. As a family, we embraced the new, healthy lifestyle of being active and nourishing our bodies in the right ways, and we realized that living healthier made us happier.

So, did I discover a new and revolutionary way of living and eating? Not exactly. I just discovered that the successful way I was eating has a name in the United States: clean eating. The core of this way of eating is about consuming fresh fruits and vegetables, high-quality meat and dairy, fewer processed foods, and more home-cooked meals. My meals became smaller and my main hydration was water. I replaced most white-flour foods with whole-wheat and ancient grains, such as quinoa and buckwheat. The super-sized cuts of meats were nowhere to be found at dinnertime. Rather, our plates were filled with rainbows of veggies, wonderful whole grains, and just the right amount of lean meats and good fats. Exercise became a daily routine in our household, and weekends were filled with outdoor play and walks with kids, just like what I remembered from when I was little.

The mental and physical benefits that I experienced in my own life, and my desire to help people feel the way I do, led me to return to school to become a nutrition and health coach. My love for cooking, eating clean, and feeding my family well deepened even more.

At the beginning of our newly found lifestyle, I tried to find a way to "healthify" all the meals we loved. Chicken Parm was now baked instead of fried, meatballs were made with turkey instead of pork, and high-sugar sodas were replaced with homemade iced teas. Little by little, the new foods that we started eating, and the new recipes we were making, became our favorites. Even more, seeing how clean eating affected me on the deepest level helped make this way of living a lifestyle and not another fad diet.

Because of our busy lives, our meals are often rushed, and we eat standing up or on the go. When we get into this kind of routine, meals become a chore and just fuel. But there are so many benefits to sitting down, chewing food well, and connecting with loved ones at the dinner table. I've found that not rushing meals helps us develop a better relationship with food. Getting a meal on the table in less than 30 minutes gives me that extra time to actually sit down and enjoy the meal, bond with my kids, or even squeeze in a workout.

In this book, I've simplified my favorite clean recipes and made them more accessible. Each recipe contains only 5 ingredients, ensuring a quick prep time, but the ingredients are carefully chosen, including locally sourced, whole, fresh foods; clean pantry items; and wonderful, aromatic spices.

I hope this cookbook inspires you to leap into the world of clean eating, one recipe at a time. I want you to find joy in cooking and realize how simple and fun mealtime can be, as you discover wonderful new recipes that leave you feeling great. The ultimate goal is to become the best and healthiest version of yourself, because you deserve it.

CHAPTER ONE

EATING CLEAN EVERY DAY

In this chapter, we will explore the building blocks of clean eating. Clean eating is not a diet, but rather a conscious lifestyle choice. With clean eating, the focus is brought back to simple meal preparations using whole, real foods in which quality supersedes quantity. Adding superfoods to your meals will ensure nutrient-dense meals that keep you satiated and happy.

It's not difficult to eat clean, and this chapter will show you how to get started. You'll want to clean out your pantry and refrigerator and restock them with healthier choices—an important step that needs to be taken when adopting this lifestyle. You'll become efficient at grocery shopping and know how to pick the right produce, which will make day-to-day clean eating even more manageable.

By the end of this first chapter, you will have all the tools you need in order to start your new clean eating lifestyle, one recipe at a time.

WHAT DOES "CLEAN EATING" REALLY MEAN?

Eating clean is a lifestyle choice we make. It's a decision to nourish our body the right way so it can thrive. It is the opportunity we give to our body to feel energized, light and healthy. It is what our bodies deserve.

I'm excited for you to explore the world of real, whole foods and bring them to your kitchen. By doing so, you will discover some of the wonderful benefits of plants, plant-based proteins, and superfoods, and realize how magically they come together in the meals you will prepare. Did I mention that these clean eating recipes are so simple, you will spend more time enjoying the meals than preparing them? That's the best part, if you ask me! With our already busy lives, we don't want to spend a ton of time in the kitchen, but would rather use that time to do something else that feeds the soul, such as going out for a walk, reading a book, watching a good movie, or spending time with loved ones.

Another bonus: When you eat clean, your sleep improves. The whole foods we eat work in synergy and they support our body's natural processes. Nourishing yourself well during the day will help you settle in better at night and support your natural sleep cycle. When you wake up feeling rested, this will be a true game-changer when it comes to conquering your day. More focus, less brain fog, and sharper and clearer thinking are just some of the benefits you will experience.

Being physically active is a big part of healthy living, and you will soon see how this new clean eating lifestyle will impact your performance in a way you may have not experienced before. Powering up your day with real food and superfoods will elevate your energy and bring out the best in you. Your body will be supported every step of the way, and you will be able to see the difference in the activities you take part in every day. Moving with ease and lightness will feel wonderful.

Another benefit of eating clean is that you can achieve your health goals by eating wonderful, nourishing meals without feeling restricted. The food you eat will be just that—food—and not some number. You'll see food as a source of life that is meant to be enjoyed. There will be no good foods or bad foods; there will be no schedules telling you what to eat and when. You are the one in charge: you and your body. When you surround yourself with nutritious foods, all you need to do is listen to the cues. Your body will tell you what works and what doesn't. You tune in and all the noise will tune out. It is truly that simple!

Clean eating has changed my life and I am thrilled for you to experience the same. Your newly found lifestyle will become second nature and will bring another level of happiness to your life.

LIVING YOUR BEST LIFE, 5 INGREDIENTS AT A TIME

Anytime I am facing something that seems difficult, I step back, reset, and go back to basics. Sometimes we make things more difficult than they really are. We take the longer road when there's a shortcut to the same destination. The same goes with food.

Healthy eating doesn't have to be complicated. It's all about working with simple ingredients and making them work together. You start with a few real, whole-food ingredients, add a couple of basic spices, and create a meal. Perhaps next time, you feel a little creative and adventurous, so you add something extra. That's wonderful, too! But overall, think clean, basic, and simple.

With our busy lives, it's hard to keep up with long recipes that have 20 ingredients and take over an hour to make. We simply don't always have that kind of time, and that is why we either choose not to cook or end up cooking, but then rush through the meal. We also end up resenting the whole idea of cooking at home, because it is such a chore.

A sustainable, healthy, clean eating lifestyle calls for simplicity and ease of meal preparation. In order to bring back joy to the kitchen, the focus needs to be on a few good-quality, easily sourced ingredients and quick preparation time. With this type of thinking, maintaining a healthy-living lifestyle in the long run can easily be achieved.

QUALITY OVER QUANTITY

Clean eating does not mean you need to let go of your favorite dishes. Most traditional meals can be modified just a bit and become more nutrient-dense so you can enjoy them on a regular basis. For example, plant-based sources of protein such as tofu, beans, lentils, and quinoa can be added to make meals healthier and more nutritious. Similarly, serving more lean cuts of meat and seafood will help reduce consumption of high-fat red meats.

Think about classic pasta Bolognese, for example. Although the traditional version is made with pork or beef and served with spaghetti, the clean, modified version is made with turkey and served with zoodles, whole-grain pasta, or quinoa. So why is the second option healthier? We replaced the pasta with more nutrient-dense options that contain more plant-based protein and fiber. As such, this meal will keep you full longer and make you just as happy as the traditional version.

How about lasagna? Can that be "healthified" a little bit, too? Of course it can! Traditional lasagna uses regular lasagna sheets, highly processed mozzarella cheese, ground pork or beef, as well as white flour for the béchamel sauce. The clean version of lasagna can be made with lentil-pasta lasagna sheets, ricotta cheese (or non-dairy, almond-milk cheese), ground turkey or tofu, and roasted veggies. While the first option is delicious, the second one is much more nutritious and can taste just as good.

If we focus on real, whole foods and good-quality meats and dairy products, clean eating becomes easy. These new simplified recipes are quick to make and much more nutritious. This will reflect in the way you feel, as you fuel your body to run optimally. Clean eating will affect your energy levels, your sleep, and your mood—all for the better!

Picking Prime Produce

Ideally, we want to try to eat locally sourced and in-season produce as much as possible. Seasonal fruits and vegetables taste better and are at their prime nutritionally. Think about it: Produce that is grown elsewhere and imported goes through many levels of handling before it actually gets to us.

I love the idea of farm shares in which you buy in for the whole season of farm-fresh fruits and veggies. Typically, the farm will offer you a small, medium, or large share and determine the days when you can go and pick up your fruits and veggies. Farms also bring their produce to farmers' markets, where you can go and make your selections on a weekly or daily basis.

Alternatively, you can shop for seasonal produce at your local grocer in the early morning for the best picks. Check with the store managers; usually the in-season produce will be from your local area.

The recipes I created for you in this book are easily adaptable to seasonal changes, so you can cook from this book year-round. Some suggestions:

Summer berries: Replace with apples or pears in the fall.

Zucchini: Replace with winter squash, acorn squash, or pumpkin in the fall.

Baby potatoes: Replace with red bliss potatoes in the fall.

Cauliflower: Replace with other cruciferous veggies such as broccoli.

Cabbage: Replace with kale.

Spring onion: Replace with yellow or red onions.

SUPERFOODS TO THE RESCUE

Not all foods are created equal. While some foods, like white flour, contain little nutritional value; others, like some of the superfoods listed below, are so nutritionally dense that they provide abundant health benefits.

Avocado: Avocados are a great source of good fats; vitamins C, E, and K; B vitamins; folate; and potassium. If you are vegetarian or vegan, avocado is a wonderful source of plant-based protein and fiber.

Berries: Packed with antioxidants, berries make a great high-fiber snack as well as a natural sweetener for healthier baking.

Beets: A true powerhouse, beets are rich in antioxidants and are anti-inflammatory. Beets contain good amounts of vitamin A and C, B_6 and folate, iron, and magnesium. This superfood is one of the best foods for immune system support.

Broccoli: The vitamin and mineral profile is similar to dark leafy greens, but broccoli contains even more fiber and protein. In fact, broccoli contains more protein than red meat! Broccoli is also packed with antioxidants.

Cabbage: This cruciferous vegetable contains high amounts of indole-3-carbinol, an antioxidant that helps fight cancer-causing free radicals. If there's one vegetable that we all need to be eating, it's this one!

Celery: Celery is a great anti-inflammatory food. It's rich in vitamins A and K, as well as potassium. Celery aids in digestive health, making it a wonderful add-in to green juices, soups, and stews.

Chia: Rich in calcium, iron, and magnesium, this superfood makes a great addition to yogurt and smoothie bowls and jams. Chia seeds contain high amounts of fiber and are great for digestive health.

Coconut: This superfood is great for digestive health, balancing blood sugar levels, and brain health. Coconut meat is rich in medium-chain triglycerides (MCTs), which are natural energy boosters. Adding coconut to your pre-workout smoothies is a great natural way to enhance your workout without taking any unhealthy, store-bought pre-workout enhancers.

Dark leafy greens (such as kale, spinach, and collard greens): These wonderful greens are rich in essential vitamins such as A, C, E, and K, vitamin B_6 and folate, as well as iron, potassium, and magnesium. Dark leafy greens are also a great source of antioxidants, plant-based protein, and fiber.

Flaxseed: This favorite oatmeal addition of mine is a great source of calcium, magnesium, and iron. This superfood is a must if you follow a vegan diet.

Ginger: I call this superfood "turmeric's cousin" because it comes from the same family as turmeric. Just like its counterpart, ginger is anti-inflammatory, anti-viral, and cleansing. The Turmeric Ginger Latte (page 170) is a delicious way to combine the two.

Oats: High in antioxidants and dietary fiber, oats help stabilize blood sugar levels. They also help with fullness, weight management, and healthy cholesterol levels. Beta glucans found in oat bran (the outer shell of oats) are great immunity boosters.

Olive oil: This superfood is rich in monounsaturated fats that keep our hearts healthy, keep cholesterol in check (by lowering triglycerides), help keep blood sugar levels stable, and improve insulin resistance, all of which contribute to a healthy weight.

Pumpkin seeds: Similar to walnuts, pumpkin seeds are high in polyunsaturated fats and rich in protein and fiber, as well as iron and magnesium. They're great salad toppers.

Quinoa: Quinoa contains the full profile of amino acids, making it a complete protein (unlike other grains). Because of its high fiber content, this gluten-free grain is absorbed slowly, resulting in more stable and sustained energy levels throughout the day.

Salmon: The essential fatty acids in this fish are great for our internal health and our skin. The omega-3s and vitamin B_{12} (cobalamin) in salmon aid in brain health, so having this type of fish as part of our diet is especially important as we age.

Turmeric: One of the strongest antioxidants, turmeric has been used in Ayurveda and traditional Chinese medicine for thousands of years. It's great in soups and stews (check out recipes on pages 113, 162, and 170.)

Walnuts: This superfood contains high amounts of omega-6 and omega-3 fatty acids, which fight inflammation and heart disease. Walnuts are high in filling fiber and protein.

THE CLEAN PANTRY

A clean pantry is one of the building blocks of clean eating. In this section, you will find a list of the essential items that you'll want to stock your pantry with. Having these foods on hand will make your clean eating lifestyle much more sustainable.

FRESH AND PERISHABLE

- **Nuts and seeds:** Choose unsalted kinds and buy in bulk. I recommend almonds, walnuts, cashews, pine nuts, pumpkin seeds, and sesame seeds.

- **Flaxseed and ground flax:** Buy in smaller quantities, as these are best when fresh.

- **Chia seeds:** Same as flax; buy smaller amounts.

- **Plant-based milks:** Unsweetened almond, oat, or cashew milk; sweetened varieties hide a lot of unnecessary sugar.

- **Nut butters/tahini/sunflower butter:** Read the back label to ensure there are no added oils. Nut butter should contain only nuts and perhaps some salt. The same is true of seed butters. Sun butter and tahini are wonderful alternatives to nut butters for those with nut allergies. Try to use them in baking; they work really well for healthy desserts.

- **Oats/oat bran:** Choose steel-cut or rolled oats. Steel-cut oats have more of a chewy, nutty texture when cooked; rolled oats are softer and cook faster. Oat bran is the outer part of the oat and contains the most fiber—it's great to add to smoothies and even oatmeal bowls.

- **Flours:** Choose smaller bags of organic flours such as spelt, whole-grain, einkorn, oat, cassava, corn, and almond. You don't need to have all the varieties in the pantry, but choose one regular flour to have on hand, such as spelt (I like this one because it's high in protein), and one gluten-free one, such as almond or oat.

- **Good-quality oils/ghee:** Choose good-quality, cold-pressed olive oil for cooking and salad dressings. Coconut oil is great for healthy baking and high-heat panfrying. Ghee, which is clarified butter, is a great lactose-free alternative to traditional butter and gives wonderful flavor to egg dishes and vegetables.

- **High-fiber crackers/rice cakes:** When choosing crackers, you'll want to be mindful of ingredients. Choose nutrient-dense crackers that contain a good amount of protein and fiber. Rice cakes are a great bread alternative to enjoy with nut butters, spreads, or your favorite sandwich toppings.

SPICES

Spices bring so much flavor to meals, elevating a simple food to something special, so go ahead and experiment with them.

As you get more comfortable with these recipes, you'll want to start experimenting with spices to take the flavors of the food even further. To help guide you, I've listed spice blends to the right of some ingredient lists. This leaves you space to explore and adjust according to your taste.

In this cookbook, we'll use spices to get the best out of the main 5 ingredients we are using in each recipe. While some dishes use only a couple of spices, others require more. If you stock your pantry with the following dried spices, you'll be all set to integrate a variety of flavors at any time.

Seasoning Plant-Based Dishes and Beyond

Once we get to the plant-based dishes, you will see that some recipes will have as many as four or five spices. Sure, you can make these dishes with just salt and pepper, but if you want to create a flavorful dish that you enjoy making and eating over and over again, you'll find that you want to add more spices. But you won't need to spend any extra time cooking or preparing. If you've already got these spices in your pantry, you can just season and serve.

This book calls for the following spices, so use these lists as a guide when you are stocking your spice rack.

For cooking:
- Basil
- Bay leaves
- Black pepper
- Cumin
- Dried onion flakes
- Garlic powder
- Gochugaru
  (Korean chili flakes)
- Ground ginger
- Himalayan salt
- Mexican chili powder
- Mint flakes
- Onion powder
- Oregano
- Parsley
- Red paprika
- Sesame seeds
- Thyme
- Turmeric powder

For baking:
- Baking soda
- Baking powder
- Ground cinnamon
- Vanilla extract

USING SPICE BLENDS

I created these special spice blends for this cookbook that I hope you will enjoy and use in many recipes besides the ones in the book.

TACO SEASONING
3 tablespoons cumin
2 tablespoons Mexican chili powder
1 tablespoon red paprika
1 teaspoon garlic powder
2 teaspoon oregano
2 teaspoons of Himalayan salt

MEDITERRANEAN BLEND
2 tablespoons basil
2 tablespoons oregano
1 tablespoon lemon zest
1 teaspoon Himalayan salt
1 teaspoon garlic powder

HEALING IMMUNE BLEND
¼ teaspoon turmeric
¼ teaspoon ginger
¼ teaspoon garlic powder
¼ teaspoon Himalayan salt

CANNED GOODS

Canned beans: Dried beans take a long time to cook, so buying cooked beans in a can and doctoring them up is a much faster alternative. Always buy varieties packed in water with no salt.

Canned tomatoes: When tomatoes are in season, buy them fresh, and when not, turn to canned. I find that plum or San Marzano tomatoes taste the best.

Canned chickpeas: These are one of my favorites to have on hand. Just drain and rinse, add to salads, and you're done.

Canned tuna: Skipjack tuna is one of my favorites; it tastes wonderful and contains very little mercury. Buy two kinds: one in water and one in olive oil.

Chicken or vegetable broth: Try to buy organic, low-sodium varieties without any additives, made with real food ingredients. Ready-made broths can be added to soups and stews to develop deeper flavors.

Tomato sauce: While it is wonderful to make your own tomato sauce, when you need a meal on the table fast, a canned one works great.

DRY GOODS

Lentils: Buy orange lentils for stews and green lentils for salads and sides.

Pasta/lasagna noodles: With a long shelf life, pastas are a food you can always keep a variety of in your pantry. Choose high-protein pastas made with spelt flour, lentils, or beans, or easily digestible pastas made with rice flour. Whole-grain pastas are wonderful as well, if you like the more rustic flavors.

Quinoa: Buy in bulk for better affordability. I like to buy white, red, and black and mix them into three-color quinoa.

Rice: Choose aromatic kinds such as jasmine or basmati or simple brown rice. Always wash well and rinse until water comes out clean.

THE CLEAN REFRIGERATOR AND FREEZER

Keeping your refrigerator and freezer well stocked and organized is as important as the clean pantry. When you surround yourself with healthy options and readily available foods, quick and healthy meals come together quickly.

THE REFRIGERATOR

Prepared veggies: Pre-washed greens such as spinach, kale, lettuce mixes, shredded carrots, pre-cut peppers, carrot and celery sticks. Although it's a little more expensive to buy pre-cut and pre-washed veggies, there is more chance you will end up eating them because you don't have to take time to wash, chop, etc.

Cruciferous veggies: Broccoli, cabbage, and cauliflower have a slightly longer shelf life, so stock up on more than one variety.

Seasonal veggies: Tomatoes, cucumbers, butter lettuce, zucchini, peppers and the like; buy as you need them. These items do not have a long shelf life, so use them first.

Good-quality dairy: Buy organic, pasture-raised, or free-range eggs (the cage-free label can be misleading). Stock up on less processed cheeses such as sheep feta, goat cheese, ricotta, or cottage cheese; buy organic Greek yogurt and plant-based yogurts such as those made with cashew or almond milk.

Condiments: Unless you use them quickly, buy smaller jars of condiments so they are always fresh. Dijon and regular yellow mustards are great to have, as well as rice and white-wine vinegar. For Asian-inspired dishes, buy soy or teriyaki sauce (ensure labels state non-GMO).

Ready-made spreads: Different healthy spreads make snacking so easy. Buy hummus or harissa (ajvar or red pepper spread) for serving with cut-up peppers, celery, or crackers.

THE FREEZER

Frozen vegetables have the same nutritional value as fresh ones. Here are some staples to keep around:

Frozen peas and string beans: Try to buy fresh peas while in season, but turn to frozen once the season is over. They have the same great flavor.

Frozen corn: Whether as a side dish or added to salad, frozen corn is a good freezer staple.

Frozen stir-fry mix: Sometimes we don't have time to shop for, prepare, and cut up seven different types of veggies. Veggie mixes such as stir-fry mix come in handy.

Frozen berries: I love buying frozen berries when berry season is over. They're much sweeter than the imported berries you find at the stores off-season.

Overripe bananas: Once bananas start to turn brown, it's a great time to freeze them. You can use them in smoothies and to make cold desserts, such as Banana Nice-Cream (page 176).

Elevate Meals with Fresh Herbs

Just like spices, fresh herbs are a great way to "spice up" the ingredients used in cooking. Simple baked chicken breast is so much more flavorful and special when you add some olive oil and freshly chopped oregano and basil on top; baked beans are richer in taste when cooked with a fresh bay leaf and topped with fresh parsley.

Fresh herbs also carry many health benefits, including polyphenols, which have anti-inflammatory and antioxidant effects and can protect us against many illnesses.

You'll want to buy fresh herbs only when you need them because they don't last as long as dried herbs do. Any use of fresh herbs in this book will either be counted toward the 5 ingredients or listed as an option.

Where Chemicals and Toxins Hide

The food industry and their suppliers do not always have our health in mind, so we need to use caution when selecting our pantry items, produce, and even packaging. Here are some common places where toxins hide:

Pesticides on fruits and vegetables: With conventionally grown produce, chemicals and pesticides are used to fight off the bad bugs and keep the vegetables and fruits healthy-looking. Some fruits and veggies with very thin skin absorb those pesticides, and when we eat that produce, we are also consuming the chemicals that were used. Conversely, organic farmers use natural products to support their crops, so when you can, it's best to buy organic. Recognizing that budget can limit us, I like to use the "Dirty Dozen" and "Clean Fifteen" lists from the Environmental Working Group (EWG) to decide what produce is most critical when it comes to organic. A couple of examples are strawberries and spinach—they are on the Dirty Dozen list every year—so those are best if organic. On the other hand, veggies with thicker skin (like eggplant), or fruits that need to be peeled (like oranges), tend to be okay if conventional.

Here is EWG's Dirty Dozen and Clean Fifteen for 2020:

DIRTY DOZEN

Strawberries	Apples	Pears
Spinach	Grapes	Tomatoes
Kale	Peaches	Celery
Nectarines	Cherries	Potatoes

CLEAN FIFTEEN

Avocado	Sweet peas (frozen)	Broccoli
Sweet corn	Eggplant	Mushrooms
Pineapple	Asparagus	Cabbage
Onions	Cauliflower	Honeydew melon
Papaya	Cantaloupe	Kiwi

BPA (bisphenol A): This chemical can be found inside the linings of cans and in plastic food-storage containers. When buying canned goods, ensure that the lining of the can is BPA-free. You can find this information on the label of the product, but if you buy organic, it is always BPA-free because organic certification requires it to be. Food storage containers are best if they're made of glass, especially if you will be putting warm food into them. When you use plastic containers, if the plastic contains BPA, the chemical can leach into the food when the warm food heats the plastic. When you can, buy pantry items in glass jars and glass bottles, and use glass storage containers.

GMOs (genetically modified organisms): When certain foods are grown (mainly soy, corn, and wheat), their natural state can be altered through genetic-engineering techniques, making them GMOs. Furthermore, these genetically modified plants are sprayed with different herbicides such as glyphosates, which have been found to be toxic for humans. Eating foods that have been derived this way is not optimal for our health and should be avoided. The greatest concern in the United States regarding GMOs is corn and soy. When buying soy- and corn-based products, ensure that the packaging clearly states non-GMO. If you buy organic, it will be non-GMO by default.

HOW TO USE THIS BOOK

The goal of this cookbook is to make clean eating practical and more manageable—for that reason, all the recipes in this book contain only 5 main ingredients, not including salt, pepper, oil, or water. The recipes include easily sourced ingredients that are versatile, in that you can easily swap them for other ingredients as the seasons change. The spices in this book are used to enhance the flavor of the ingredients, and because you'll have these in your pantry as staples, they'll be easy to add to your recipes when you want to take flavors up a notch.

Although this book promises 5-ingredient recipes, you won't want to stop there. When you see how easy and impactful it can be to add a few herbs or spices, you'll want to do more. That's why a few recipes also contain a *secondary* ingredient list. Using the spices in the *Spice It Up!* lists will elevate your meals to the next level, so I highly encourage you to use them all.

I've also included serving tips with additional ingredient ideas. This way, you can build on the depth of flavor and texture, and with that, raise the enjoyment level of these dishes.

When you cook, I encourage you to think about the ingredients you are using, where they came from, and how wonderfully nourishing they are. Recipe by recipe, you will discover how simple cooking can be and how flavorful and enjoyable clean food can be.

TIPS

Here are some helpful tips that will be featured with the recipes:

Prep tip: Cooking or baking tips, tips for cutting ingredients a certain way or for more efficient preparation

Ingredient tip: How to get the most out of a particular ingredient

Substitution tip: How to replace an ingredient with something else

Seasonal tip: Suggestions for adding or changing ingredients as seasons change to embrace the flavors and freshness of in-season ingredients

Storage tip: How to properly store leftovers, as well as partially used ingredients such as dressings

Serving tip: How to add ingredients or garnishes to further elevate the flavor or nutrition of a dish

Homemade Granola
page 18

CHAPTER TWO

BREAKFASTS

A good night's sleep and a nutritious and filling breakfast set the tone for a successful day ahead. Morning routines can also ensure that your morning doesn't feel rushed. Set your alarm clock to wake a little earlier and prepare yourself a nice, well-balanced breakfast from the recipes in this chapter. Then sit down and enjoy it with your favorite morning drink, such as coffee, tea, or green juice. The recipes you will find in this chapter are not just recipes for breakfast, but also recipes for feeling good throughout the day.

* Homemade Granola 18

Classic Cinnamon Oatmeal 19

Oatmeal with Baked Apples and Walnuts 20

Coconut Oat Bran 21

Overnight Chia and Quinoa Pudding with Coconut 22

Yogurt Chia Pudding 23

Overnight Chia Pudding with Berries 24

Scrambled Tofu 25

Omelet with Spinach and Goat Cheese 26

Shakshuka 27

Baked Sunny-Side Up Eggs with Zoodles 29

Veggie Egg Muffins 30

American Protein Pancakes 31

Protein Waffles with Spinach 32

Savory Corn Muffins with Spinach and Feta 33

HOMEMADE GRANOLA

DAIRY-FREE · GLUTEN-FREE · SOY-FREE · VEGAN
Prep time: 5 minutes · **Cook time:** 15 minutes
Yield: 15 ounces

Making your own granola is very easy and much healthier than the store-bought variety, which tends to be low in protein and fiber, and high in sugar or even high-fructose corn syrup. There are many wonderful ways to eat granola, but my favorite is with some Greek yogurt, fresh berries, and a drizzle of honey. You can also enjoy this granola with plant-based milk, such as almond or oat, and some fresh raspberries. Sprinkling some granola on Banana Nice-Cream (page 176) adds a crunchy touch of deliciousness, too.

1 cup rolled oats
1 cup walnuts
½ cup shredded coconut
¼ cup maple syrup
¼ cup coconut oil

1. Preheat the oven to 400°F.
2. In a bowl, mix the oats, walnuts, and shredded coconut thoroughly, then set aside.
3. In a small saucepan, combine the maple syrup and coconut oil and bring just to a boil.
4. Pour the warm maple and coconut oil mixture over the dry mixture. Mix to combine.
5. Spread the granola in a single layer on a baking sheet lined with parchment paper.
6. Bake for 15 minutes.
7. Let the granola cool completely before storing it in a glass container with a lid.

* **Prep tip:** Granola is great to prepare on a Sunday for enjoying during the week. You can also pre-portion the granola in single-serving-size snack containers to take on the go.

* **Substitution tip:** You can use any type of nut for this granola. Almonds and hazelnuts work great. You can also use sunflower seeds if you wish to make the granola nut-free. Honey can be used instead of maple syrup, too.

Per serving (3 ounces): Calories: 389; Fat: 30g; Protein: 7g; Carbohydrates: 27g; Fiber: 4g; Sodium: 4mg

CLASSIC CINNAMON OATMEAL

DAIRY-FREE • GLUTEN-FREE • NUT-FREE • SOY-FREE • VEGAN
Prep time: 5 minutes • **Cook time:** 20 minutes
Yield: 4 servings

Steel-cuts oats have a wonderful nutty texture that complements a variety of toppings. For warmer days, dress them up with berries and honey and cook them in water. For colder days, add banana, walnuts, and maple syrup, and cook them in almond milk. On days when you need extra protein, cook the oats and add whey or a plant-based protein of your choice.

2 cups water
1 cup steel-cut oats
½ teaspoon cinnamon
½ teaspoon vanilla extract
1 tablespoon flaxseed

1. In a small saucepan, bring the water to a boil.
2. Add the oats, cinnamon, and vanilla; reduce heat to low; cover, and cook for about 20 minutes.
3. Remove from heat, stir in the flaxseed, cover again, and let rest for 5 minutes.
4. Add toppings of choice and serve warm.

✱ **Prep tip:** Oatmeal is great for meal preps. Cook a double batch and simply store it in a covered glass container in the refrigerator for up to 5 days. When serving, just add some warm almond milk or heat it up in the microwave.

Per serving: Calories: 176; Fat: 3g; Protein: 5g; Carbohydrates: 32g; Fiber: 5g; Sodium: 1mg

OATMEAL WITH BAKED APPLES AND WALNUTS

DAIRY-FREE · GLUTEN-FREE · SOY-FREE · VEGAN
Prep time: 5 minutes · **Cook time:** 20 minutes
Yield: 4 servings

The smell of baked apples and cinnamon reminds me of my childhood. It was a dessert my brother and I loved and ate often. One year, during apple-picking season, I decided to bake the apples the way I remembered them while growing up, so I added them to a warm bowl of hearty oats. The result was magical! Apple pie for breakfast, anyone?

2 apples, peeled, cored, and halved
Coconut oil spray (optional)
1 teaspoon cinnamon
2 cups water
1 cup steel-cut oats
4 tablespoons chopped walnuts

1. Preheat the oven to 375°F.
2. Spread the apples cut-side up on a small baking sheet, then spray with coconut oil (if using), and sprinkle with cinnamon.
3. Bake 15 minutes, or until tender.
4. Meanwhile, in a small saucepan, bring the water to a boil.
5. Add the oats, reduce heat to low, cover, and cook for about 20 minutes.
6. Remove from heat and set aside.
7. In each of 4 serving bowls, add a quarter of the oatmeal, ½ apple, and sprinkle a tablespoon of walnuts on top.

* **Ingredient tip:** Pears work well in this recipe, too, but cooking time may be longer. When apples are in season, you can bake a big batch, pack them in individual serving-size containers and freeze them. Take them out of the freezer the night before you want to eat them, and warm them up in the oven the next day.

Per serving: Calories: 248; Fat: 7g; Protein: 6g; Carbohydrates: 43g; Fiber: 6g; Sodium: 0mg

COCONUT OAT BRAN

DAIRY-FREE • GLUTEN-FREE • NUT-FREE • SOY-FREE • VEGAN

Prep time: 5 minutes

Yield: 1 serving

Oat bran is the outer layer of the oat groat; that is, the first edible part of the oat grain. Oat bran contains more protein and fiber than oats, is rich in antioxidants, and is a great source of magnesium, zinc, and iron, as well as vitamin B_6, folate, and calcium. The texture is similar to that of rolled oats; softer and less chewy than steel-cut oats. As such, oat bran doesn't need to be cooked, but rather soaked for a few minutes in a hot liquid of choice.

1 cup unsweetened coconut milk
½ cup oat bran
1 teaspoon ground flaxseed
1 tablespoon coconut protein

1. In a small saucepan, bring the coconut milk to a boil.
2. Meanwhile, in a serving bowl, combine the oat bran, ground flaxseed, and coconut protein, and stir to blend.
3. Remove the hot coconut milk from the stove and pour it over the oat bran mixture.
4. Stir well to combine. Let rest for about 5 minutes or until the mixture starts to thicken.
5. Enjoy warm.

* **Substitution tip:** You can replace coconut milk with any other type of plant-based milk, such as unsweetened almond, rice, or oat milk.

Per serving: Calories: 305; Fat: 9g; Protein: 17g; Carbohydrates: 55g; Fiber: 10g; Sodium: 92mg

OVERNIGHT CHIA AND QUINOA PUDDING WITH COCONUT

DAIRY-FREE · GLUTEN-FREE · SOY-FREE · VEGAN

Prep time: 5 minutes
Yield: 2 servings

There are many easy ways to add the superfood chia to your meal repertoire, such as adding it to smoothies, making chia pudding, tossing it on top of salads, or adding it to oats or quinoa bowls as I did in this recipe.

¼ cup chia seeds
1⅛ cups vanilla almond milk
6 tablespoons crunchy quinoa
2 dates, pitted and finely chopped
3 tablespoons unsweetened shredded coconut

1. In a glass bowl, mix together the chia seeds and vanilla almond milk, stirring well.
2. Add the quinoa, chopped dates, and shredded coconut. Stir to combine.
3. Cover and refrigerate overnight. Enjoy in the morning!

* **Ingredient tip:** You can use plain, unsweetened almond milk in place of vanilla almond milk; just add ½ teaspoon of vanilla extract or ½ teaspoon of maple syrup.

* **Substitution tip:** You can use leftover cooked quinoa instead of crunchy quinoa. The taste will remain the same.

Per serving: Calories: 355; Fat: 15g; Protein: 10g; Carbohydrates: 48g; Fiber: 14g; Sodium: 93mg

YOGURT CHIA PUDDING

GLUTEN-FREE • NUT-FREE • SOY-FREE • VEGETARIAN

Prep time: 5 minutes
Yield: 1 serving

This recipe makes a healthy and nutritious breakfast, but it also makes a wonderful dessert or snack. I suggest using full-fat, organic Greek yogurt here because the more fat the yogurt contains, the creamier the pudding will be. Although this breakfast is light on flavors, it delivers great nutrition, and with its high amounts of protein, fiber, and omega-3s, this chia pudding will keep you satiated and happy for many hours to come.

1 (6-ounce) container plain Greek yogurt
3 tablespoons chia seeds
1 tablespoon maple syrup
½ teaspoon vanilla extract

1. Combine the yogurt, chia seeds, maple syrup, and vanilla in a glass bowl or jar with a lid.
2. Stir until well combined.
3. Cover and let rest for about 20 minutes on the kitchen counter or in the refrigerator.
4. Mix and add your favorite fruit toppings, if desired.

✳ **Prep tip:** You can also refrigerate this pudding overnight in a portable food storage container so it's ready when you wake up first thing in the morning. This is great for busy mornings or to take to the office or school.

Per serving: Calories: 368; Fat: 19g; Protein: 13g; Carbohydrates: 40g; Fiber: 15g; Sodium: 88mg

OVERNIGHT CHIA PUDDING WITH BERRIES

GLUTEN-FREE · NUT-FREE · SOY-FREE · VEGETARIAN

Prep time: 5 minutes
Yield: 2 servings

Berries are truly nature's candy! Tasty and packed with antioxidants, berries make a wonderful snack, and adding them to your breakfast makes the start of the day even sweeter. During the summer, enjoy berries at their ripest, and during the fall and winter months buy them frozen. You'll still reap all the benefits because the nutrients remain the same. Raspberries and strawberries contain the natural sugar fructose, making them a perfect food when your body wants something sweet. Raspberries and strawberries are high in dietary fiber, which ensures slower absorption of the sugar into the bloodstream, helping to keep blood sugar levels stable.

2 tablespoons fresh or frozen berries
1 cup vanilla almond milk yogurt
¼ cup chia seeds
2 tablespoons crushed cashews
1 tablespoon cacao powder

1. If using fresh berries, mash them. Combine the berries, yogurt, chia seeds, cashews, and cacao in a glass bowl or glass jar with a lid.
2. Stir until well combined and refrigerate overnight.
3. Mix before enjoying.

* **Substitution tip:** You can use any berries of your choice. I typically use a mix of frozen strawberries, raspberries, and blueberries.

Per serving: Calories: 290; Fat: 20g; Protein: 11g; Carbohydrates: 23g; Fiber: 13g; Sodium: 34mg

SCRAMBLED TOFU

DAIRY-FREE · GLUTEN-FREE · NUT-FREE · VEGAN

Prep time: 10 minutes · **Cook time:** 10 minutes
Yield: 2 servings

Tofu is a wonderful source of plant-based protein made from soy milk derived from soy beans. Unfortunately, more than 80 percent of the soy that is imported or grown in the United States is genetically modified, hence it is less than optimal for human consumption (see page 13). When buying tofu or other soy-based products, it's important to look for the non-GMO label or buy organic. I find that extra-firm tofu has the best texture, and it works well with scrambles like this one, as well as when you are baking or panfrying it.

1 tablespoon extra-virgin olive oil
½ green bell pepper, thinly sliced
½ yellow onion, thinly sliced
1 package extra-firm tofu, patted dry, crumbled

Spice it up:
¼ teaspoon Himalayan salt
¼ teaspoon garlic powder
¼ teaspoon cumin

1. In a small sauté pan or skillet, heat the olive oil over medium heat.
2. Add the pepper and onion, and sauté until the onion is translucent.
3. Add the crumbled tofu, and salt, garlic, and cumin (if using). Sauté for about 4 minutes, until all the flavors combine nicely.
4. Serve warm.

✳ **Ingredient tip:** Tofu usually is packaged in water, and it's important to dry it well before using it. Remove the tofu from the package and drain the water out. Wrap the tofu in triple-layered paper towels and put it in a colander to sit for 10 minutes.

Per serving: Calories: 277; Fat: 15g; Protein: 20g; Carbohydrates: 8g; Fiber: 2g; Sodium: 234mg

OMELET WITH SPINACH AND GOAT CHEESE

GLUTEN-FREE • NUT-FREE • SOY-FREE • VEGETARIAN
Prep time: 3 minutes • **Cook time:** 5 minutes
Yield: 1 serving

Omelets are a terrific breakfast option, but depending how you dress them up, they can make a great lunch or dinner as well. For breakfast, choose veggie omelets with some Greek yogurt on top. For lunch, you might choose to make one frittata style with high-fiber vegetables such as broccoli and mushrooms, and serve alongside a mixed-greens salad. For dinner, try making your omelet with leftover steak or with chicken sausage and spinach. All delicious!

1 tablespoon extra-virgin olive oil
1 scallion (green and white parts), finely chopped
1 cup baby spinach, roughly chopped
2 large eggs, beaten
¼ teaspoon Himalayan salt
Freshly ground black pepper (optional)
1 tablespoon goat cheese

Spice it up:
¼ teaspoon oregano

1. In a nonstick sauté pan or skillet over medium heat, heat the olive oil.
2. Add the scallions and sauté for about 1 minute, until wilted.
3. Add the spinach and cook for another minute.
4. Add the beaten eggs, salt, pepper, and oregano (if using). Stir to combine and cook on low heat until the bottom of the omelet seems firm.
5. Add the goat cheese and use a wide spatula to carefully fold the omelet in half.
6. Cook for 1 minute, then flip over and cook for another minute.
7. Serve warm.

✳ **Prep tip:** The key to a fluffy omelet is not beating the eggs too much. Beat until just incorporated.

Per serving: Calories: 294; Fat: 25g; Protein: 15g; Carbohydrates: 3g; Fiber: 1g; Sodium: 578mg

SHAKSHUKA

GLUTEN-FREE • NUT-FREE • SOY-FREE • VEGETARIAN

Prep time: 10 minutes • **Cook time:** 10 minutes

Yield: 2 servings

If you're looking for an easy way to add more vegetables to your meals, look no further. With shakshuka, you can get creative and use any veggies you like. Think about using a rainbow and you cannot go wrong. Here we'll use three different colors of peppers and some delicious crushed San Marzano tomatoes. You can also add some basil and oregano. The sweetness of these spices tones down the acidity of the tomatoes, but at the same time they enhance the sweetness of the peppers.

3 tablespoons extra-virgin olive oil

3 bell peppers (green, yellow, red), cubed

½ yellow onion, finely chopped

½ cup crushed tomatoes

¼ teaspoon Himalayan salt

4 large eggs

¼ cup crumbled feta

Avocado (optional)

Fresh parsley (optional)

Spice it up:

¼ teaspoon oregano

¼ teaspoon basil

Freshly ground black pepper

1. In a large sauté pan or skillet over medium heat, heat the olive oil.
2. Add the peppers and onion, cover, and cook for about 2 minutes.
3. Add the crushed tomatoes and salt, and the oregano, basil, and black pepper (if using). Cover and cook until most of the liquid evaporates, about 5 minutes.
4. With a slotted spoon, move the veggies around, making 4 circles in between the veggies where you can drop in the eggs. Crack an egg into each circle and cover the pan with a lid. Cook for about 2 minutes for a runny yolk, or longer if you prefer them more well done.
5. When the eggs are done, add some crumbled feta on top. Turn off the heat, cover, and let the dish rest for 1 or 2 minutes, until the feta melts.
6. Add some avocado and fresh parsley on top (if using), and serve warm.

Continued ❯

Continued

＊ **Prep tip:** You can prepare the vegetable part of this dish (steps 1 through 3) the night before. When you're ready to enjoy this dish, just heat the vegetables and follow the recipe as directed. You can also just chop the onions and peppers and store them in a glass container in the refrigerator until ready to use.

Per serving: Calories: 467; Fat: 34g; Protein: 19g; Carbohydrates: 24g; Fiber: 4g; Sodium: 536mg

BAKED SUNNY-SIDE UP EGGS WITH ZOODLES

DAIRY-FREE • GLUTEN-FREE • NUT-FREE • SOY-FREE • VEGETARIAN

Prep time: 10 minutes • **Cook time:** 7 minutes
Yield: 1 serving

I love zucchini, but it's not the easiest vegetable to prepare unless you are making soups or stews. Because of its high water content, zucchini becomes watery and mushy fast. To prevent this when roasting or grilling zucchini, cut them and dry them with a paper towel first. Similarly, if you are spiralizing zucchini to make zoodles, it's important to take some of the water out. Prepared right, zucchini is worth the trouble; rich in vitamin C and with good amounts of vitamin B as well. With some protein and fiber and essentially no fat, zucchini pairs nicely with eggs.

2 tablespoons extra-virgin olive oil
½ small red onion, finely sliced
1 zucchini, spiralized and patted dry
¼ teaspoon Himalayan salt
2 large eggs
1 teaspoon chives, finely chopped
Freshly ground black pepper (optional)

Spice it up:
¼ teaspoon oregano

1. In a medium sauté pan or skillet over medium heat, heat the olive oil.
2. Add the onion and cook until soft and translucent.
3. Add the zucchini, oregano (if using), and salt. Sauté for 2 minutes.
4. With a slotted spoon, move the zucchini to make 2 circles where you can drop in the eggs. Add the eggs and cover. Cook for about 2 minutes for a runny yolk, or longer if you prefer them more well done.
5. Add the fresh chives and black pepper, if desired.
6. Serve immediately.

Per serving: Calories: 429; Fat: 37g; Protein: 15g; Carbohydrates: 10g; Fiber: 3g; Sodium: 549mg

VEGGIE EGG MUFFINS

DAIRY-FREE • GLUTEN-FREE • NUT-FREE • SOY-FREE • VEGETARIAN
Prep time: 6 minutes • **Cook time:** 20 minutes
Yield: 6 muffins

This recipe is a great way to add more vegetables to your clean eating. Start off by using veggies as outlined in the recipe but then go ahead and use anything you have available in the kitchen. The best part is, you can even use leftover roasted or grilled veggies as well. Simply chop them and add them in instead of the fresh veggies. As far as spices, try using Mediterranean blend (chapter 1, page 9) or just simply add oregano instead of basil. The egg muffins can be stored in the fridge in a glass container and either served cold the next day or warmed up in the microwave.

1 tablespoon extra-virgin olive oil
1 Cubanelle green pepper, chopped
1 scallion, green and white parts, finely chopped
1 cup zucchini, diced
¼ teaspoon Himalayan salt
4 large eggs, beaten

Spice it up:
¼ teaspoon dried basil
⅛ teaspoon garlic powder
¼ teaspoon red paprika (optional)

1. Preheat the oven to 400°F.
2. In a sauté pan or skillet over medium heat, heat the olive oil. Add the pepper and scallion. Sauté for about 3 minutes.
3. Add the zucchini, salt, and basil, garlic powder, and paprika (if using). Cook for another 2 minutes.
4. In 6 cups of a lined muffin pan, add the vegetables, then top each cup with an egg.
5. Bake for 20 minutes and serve immediately.

✳ **Substitution tip:** You can replace pepper and zucchini with any vegetables that you like. Spinach, kale, mushrooms, red bell peppers, asparagus, and yellow onion all work well.

Per serving (2 muffins): Calories: 150; Fat: 11g; Protein: 9g; Carbohydrates: 4g; Fiber: 1g; Sodium: 203mg

AMERICAN PROTEIN PANCAKES

DAIRY-FREE · GLUTEN-FREE · SOY-FREE · VEGETARIAN
Prep time: 3 minutes · **Cook time:** 10 minutes
Yield: 3 pancakes

Traditional American pancakes are made with white flour, buttermilk, and butter, making them not very nutritious. But substituting white flour with oat and almond flour, and buttermilk with plant-based milk, makes this family favorite rich in nutrients. In this recipe, we use baking staples such as cinnamon, vanilla extract, and baking soda. Once you have these in your pantry, they will last a while.

Coconut oil
1 large egg
1 tablespoon honey
4 tablespoons unsweetened almond milk
4 tablespoons oat flour
4 tablespoons almond flour
1 teaspoon baking soda

Spice it up:
1 teaspoon vanilla extract
1 teaspoon cinnamon

1. In a large, nonstick sauté pan or skillet over medium heat, melt the coconut oil.
2. Meanwhile, whisk together the egg, honey, milk, and vanilla (if using). Add the oat and almond flour, baking soda, and cinnamon (if using). Stir to combine.
3. Working in batches if needed, scoop the batter into 3 pancakes in the pan. Let cook until the tops bubble, then flip and cook until golden brown. Serve warm.

✳ **Prep tip:** Double the recipe and store the pancakes in a glass container in the refrigerator for up to 2 days.

✳ **Substitution tip:** I used unsweetened almond milk in this recipe, but you can use oat milk, rice milk, or cashew milk. Even vanilla-flavored, plant-based milks will work well.

✳ **Serving tip:** My favorite toppings for these pancakes are peanut butter and blueberries, or banana and cacao nibs. Adding peanut butter and banana to cold pancakes makes a delicious dessert.

Per serving: Calories: 420; Fat: 20g; Protein: 15g; Carbohydrates: 46g; Fiber: 6g; Sodium: 1320mg

PROTEIN WAFFLES WITH SPINACH

DAIRY-FREE • GLUTEN-FREE • NUT-FREE • SOY-FREE • VEGETARIAN

Prep time: 2 minutes • **Cook time:** 10 minutes

Yield: 2 waffles

These high-protein and high-fiber waffles are a wonderful option for a nutritious breakfast or snack. And the topping options are endless! I love them with vegan cream cheese, harissa (*ajvar*), or mashed avocado and chili pepper flakes. These waffles also make a great sandwich base—so much more nourishing than plain white bread slices. Just add your favorite sandwich spread, such as vegan mayo, arugula, and smoked turkey breast, and your delicious waffle sandwich is ready.

1½ tablespoons extra-virgin olive oil, divided
1 cup baby spinach
2 large eggs, beaten
½ cup almond flour
¼ cup tapioca flour
½ teaspoon baking soda
¼ teaspoon Himalayan salt

Spice it up:
¼ teaspoon oregano
¼ teaspoon garlic powder

1. In a nonstick sauté pan or skillet over medium heat, heat ½ tablespoon of olive oil.
2. Add the spinach and sauté until spinach wilts, about 3 minutes. Set aside.
3. In a bowl, combine the eggs, the remaining tablespoon of olive oil, almond flour, tapioca flour, baking soda, salt, and oregano and garlic powder (if using). Mix to blend.
4. Stir in the spinach.
5. Make the waffles according to your waffle maker instructions.

* **Substitution tip:** You can use coconut oil or ghee in this recipe instead of olive oil. You can also replace the spinach with kale or Swiss chard; you'll just need to sauté the greens a little longer.

* **Storage tip:** These waffles are great to make in advance. Store them in silicone freezer bags. When you are ready to cook just defrost them overnight or pop them in the toaster.

Per serving (1 waffle): Calories: 361; Fat: 27g; Protein: 12g; Carbohydrates: 21g; Fiber: 4g; Sodium: 554mg

SAVORY CORN MUFFINS WITH SPINACH AND FETA

GLUTEN-FREE · NUT-FREE · SOY-FREE · VEGETARIAN

Prep time: 5 minutes · **Cook time:** 20 minutes

Yield: 6 muffins

Savory corn bread is really popular in the part of Europe I come from. This bread, called *proja*, is traditionally made with white and corn flour, farmer's cheese, collard greens, and vegetable oil. It's cut in squares and served with a drinkable yogurt. I simplified the original recipe and made it more nutrient dense. These muffins make a great breakfast or snack and are also easy to take on the go.

2 cups baby spinach, roughly chopped

1½ cups fine corn flour

1 cup yogurt

2 large eggs, beaten

¼ cup crumbled feta

¼ cup olive oil

1 teaspoon baking powder

½ teaspoon Himalayan salt

1. Preheat the oven to 400°F.
2. In a mixing bowl, combine the spinach, corn flour, yogurt, eggs, feta, olive oil, baking powder, and salt, and mix well.
3. Line 6 cups of a muffin pan with silicone or paper liners.
4. Fill the cups three-quarters full with batter.
5. Bake for about 22 minutes, until a toothpick inserted in the center of a muffin comes out clean.

* **Substitution tip:** You can use ricotta or cottage cheese here as well. The spinach can be swapped with Swiss chard or kale; just chop it even finer.

* **Prep tip:** These savory muffins make a great meal-prep item. Make a double batch and store per instructions below. Warm them in the microwave or enjoy them at room temperature.

* **Storage tip:** Store in a covered glass container at room temperature for 2 days, then transfer to the refrigerator.

Per serving (1 muffin): Calories: 253; Fat: 14g; Protein: 7g; Carbohydrates: 25g; Fiber: 2g; Sodium: 221mg

Arugula Watermelon Salad
page 48

CHAPTER THREE

SOUPS, SALADS, AND DRESSINGS

Soups and salads are a great way to add more nutritionally dense foods to your daily menu. There is always space for a lovely microgreen salad or creamy veggie bisque! The soups and salads in this chapter are simple to make and big on flavor. You can mix and match them when you feel like having just soup and salad for lunch, or make any of these salads a complete main meal by adding some lean meats such as grilled chicken, turkey burger, or grass-fed steak, or some plant-based protein such as tempeh or tofu. I've also included some of my favorite dressing recipes in this chapter, which you can use with many different salads.

Creamy Broccoli Soup 37

Veggie Minestrone Soup 39

Swiss Chard Zucchini Soup 40

Spicy Tomato Bisque 41

Gluten-Free Veggie Ramen Noodle Soup 43

Butter Lettuce with Sesame Dressing 44

Traditional Greek Salad 45

Garbanzo Bean Salad 46

Roasted Beet Salad 47

* Arugula Watermelon Salad 48

Cold Bean Salad 49

Roasted Red Pepper Salad   50

Avocado Corn Salad with Tahini Dressing   51

Kale Salad with Roasted Butternut Squash   52

Arugula Salad with Baked Acorn Squash and Pomegranate Seeds   53

CREAMY BROCCOLI SOUP

GLUTEN-FREE • NUT-FREE • SOY-FREE • VEGETARIAN

Prep time: 5 minutes • **Cook time:** 25 minutes
Yield: 2 servings

This is one of the first soups I learned how to make when I started eating for my health. Broccoli was not one of the vegetables I liked, and neither was cauliflower. So, for me, this was a great way to add these two veggies to my diet in a way I enjoyed. I remember my mom making a similar soup for me when I was in college, with broccoli, potatoes, and celery, so over the years this recipe was born.

1 small head broccoli, broken into florets
½ head cauliflower, broken into florets
1 small yellow onion, cut in half
1 small carrot, chopped
1¾ teaspoons Himalayan salt
1 tablespoon Pecorino Romano cheese

Spice it up!
½ teaspoon basil

1. In a medium stockpot, combine the broccoli, cauliflower, onion, carrot, salt, basil (if using), and 6 cups of water.
2. Bring to a boil, then reduce heat to medium and simmer, covered, until the veggies are tender, about 20 minutes.
3. Using a colander, drain the water, reserving 2 cups of cooking liquid.
4. Add the vegetables to a high-speed blender with 1 cup of the reserved liquid. Carefully blend to desired consistency, working in batches, if needed. If you like bisque to be on the thinner side, add more of the reserved liquid.
5. Pour the bisque back in the pot and bring to a boil.
6. Stir in the cheese, then cover and let soup rest for 3 minutes.
7. Serve warm with some high-fiber crackers or a piece of whole-grain toast.

Continued ❯

CREAMY BROCCOLI SOUP

Continued

* **Storage tip:** This soup freezes well, so it's wonderful to prepare in big batches and store to be used later.

* **Substitution tip:** You can use low-sodium vegetable broth instead of water; just reduce the salt to ½ teaspoon or to taste. You can also replace the onion with a celery stalk and use Parmesan cheese instead of Pecorino. To make this bisque vegan, add 1 tablespoon of vegan cream cheese instead of Pecorino Romano.

* **Serving tip:** For an even creamier and more delicious soup, try adding some shredded Pecorino Romano cheese or some Greek yogurt at the very end or just before serving. Sprinkling some pumpkin seeds on top will add some extra plant-based protein and crunch. I also love adding fresh parsley.

Per serving: Calories: 106; Fat: 2g; Protein: 7g; Carbohydrates: 19g; Fiber: 7g; Sodium: 430mg

VEGGIE MINESTRONE SOUP

DAIRY-FREE • GLUTEN-FREE • NUT-FREE • SOY-FREE • VEGAN
Prep time: 5 minutes • **Cook time:** 30 minutes
Yield: 4 servings

There is nothing better than a cozy lunch with a bowl of hearty veggie soup. I love adding chickpeas or beans to soups—they add extra lean protein and make the soup a complete meal. I used some of my favorite veggies in this recipe, but you can really include any veggies you like. Broccoli is great in soups because it contains fiber and protein and adds crunch, as it doesn't cook as fast as other vegetables.

3 tablespoons extra-virgin olive oil
1 large yellow onion, thinly sliced
1 teaspoon Himalayan salt
2 medium green zucchini, cubed
1 small head broccoli, broken into small, bite-size florets
1 (13-ounce) can chickpeas, rinsed and drained
4 cups water
2½ cups tomato puree

Spice it up!
¾ to 1 teaspoon basil
¾ to 1 teaspoon oregano

1. In a medium stockpot over medium heat, heat the oil.
2. Add the onion and sauté for about 2 minutes.
3. Add the salt, and basil and oregano (if using), followed by the zucchini, broccoli, and chickpeas.
4. Add the water and tomato puree. Stir, cover, and cook on low heat for about 30 minutes, until the liquid reduces by half and the vegetables are tender.
5. Serve warm.

* **Substitution tip:** Use 1 cubed sweet potato or large carrot instead of the zucchini to make the stew a bit sweeter (just cube them smaller because they cook more slowly than zucchini). Sweet vegetables like these help balance blood sugar levels and satisfy sugar cravings.

* **Ingredient tip:** Add some red pepper flakes if you like your soup spicy.

Per serving: Calories: 313; Fat: 13g; Protein: 12g; Carbohydrates: 42g; Fiber: 12g; Sodium: 576mg

SWISS CHARD ZUCCHINI SOUP

DAIRY-FREE · GLUTEN-FREE · NUT-FREE · SOY-FREE · VEGAN
Prep time: 10 minutes · **Cook time:** 20 minutes
Yield: 2 servings as a main, 4 servings as a side

I love making this soup all year round. During the warmer months, I like adding 1 tablespoon of cold Greek yogurt to make the soup more refreshing. In winter, besides having it for lunch, I also like sipping it in the afternoon as a snack. This soup is rich in fiber and packed with antioxidants, and because it contains sweet potatoes, it keeps blood sugar in check, too.

1 small sweet potato, cut into small (½-inch) cubes
2 celery stalks, chopped
2 cups Swiss chard, chopped
1 large zucchini, chopped
1 teaspoon Himalayan salt
Freshly ground black pepper

Spice it up!
¾ to 1 teaspoon basil
¾ to 1 teaspoon oregano

1. In a large stockpot, combine the sweet potato, celery, Swiss chard, zucchini, salt, basil and oregano (if using), and 6 cups of water.
2. Bring to a boil, reduce heat to medium, and simmer until tender, about 20 minutes.
3. Using a colander, drain the water, reserving 2 cups of the cooking liquid.
4. Add the vegetables and 2 cups of water to a high-speed blender. Carefully blend to desired consistency, working in batches and covering the top with a towel to prevent spattering.
5. Pour the soup back in the stockpot and bring to a boil. Add additional salt, if needed, and black pepper to taste.

✳ **Substitution tip:** Swap the sweet potato for 1 small, chopped white potato and 1 small, chopped carrot. Spinach also works well in place of Swiss chard; just increase greens to 3 cups.

✳ **Prep tip:** This soup is great to make in big batches. You can store it in the refrigerator for up to 1 week or freeze for longer.

Per serving: Calories: 94; Fat: 1g; Protein: 4g; Carbohydrates: 20g; Fiber: 5g; Sodium: 430mg

SPICY TOMATO BISQUE

DAIRY-FREE · GLUTEN-FREE · NUT-FREE · SOY-FREE · VEGAN
Prep time: 5 minutes · **Cook time:** 15 minutes
Yield: 2 servings as a main, 4 servings as a side

"Nightshades" are vegetables that come from the plant family Solanaceae and naturally contain lectins and an alkaloid called solanine, which can be toxic in very high concentrations. Peppers, eggplant, potatoes, and tomatoes are nightshades, but they contain very low concentrations of this alkaloid. However, studies show that nightshades can cause gut irritation and inflammation in some people. Holistically, there is also a belief that because nightshades grow at night with moonlight versus sunlight these vegetables carry different energy, making them harder to metabolize. If you don't notice any effects when eating nightshades, you have nothing to worry about. Tomatoes, potatoes, peppers, and eggplant are wonderful foods that deserve a spot in clean eating!

2 tablespoons extra-virgin olive oil
1 garlic clove, quartered
1 tablespoon buckwheat flour
24 ounces tomato puree or juice
½ celery stalk, cut in half
½ teaspoon Himalayan salt

Spice it up!
1 teaspoon red paprika
¼ teaspoon red pepper flakes
½ teaspoon basil
½ teaspoon oregano

1. In a medium stockpot over low heat, heat the olive oil and add the garlic.
2. As soon as the garlic is fragrant, add the paprika and red pepper flakes.
3. Add the buckwheat flour and tomato puree. Whisk so the flour doesn't clump up.
4. Add the celery, basil, oregano, and salt.
5. Cover and cook on low, about 15 minutes.
6. Take out the garlic and celery before serving. Alternatively, you can add the bisque to a blender and carefully blend until celery and garlic are chopped.
7. Serve warm. Add 1 tablespoon of Greek yogurt when serving and some fresh parsley on top, if desired.

Continued ❯

Continued

* **Ingredient tip:** Depending what type of tomato puree/juice you buy, you may need to adjust the salt. Try to select pure tomato without sugar or salt. I love oregano flavors, so I always add some extra oregano at the end as well.

* **Substitution tip:** You can use any flour of your choice. Almond and rice flours also work well.

* **Seasonal tip:** This soup can be made any time of the year, but I suggest you try making this soup in the summer when tomatoes are in season. Farms often sell freshly made tomato puree or juice.

Per serving: Calories: 189; Fat: 14g; Protein: 3g; Carbohydrates: 15g; Fiber: 7g; Sodium: 586mg

GLUTEN-FREE VEGGIE RAMEN NOODLE SOUP

DAIRY-FREE • GLUTEN-FREE • NUT-FREE • SOY-FREE • VEGAN
Prep time: 10 minutes · **Cook time:** 20 minutes
Yield: 1 serving as a main; 2 servings as a side

Made with healing and immune boosting spices such as turmeric, ginger, and garlic, this soup will become one of your favorites. Turmeric and ginger are two of the strongest antioxidants, and both have been used in Ayurvedic and traditional Chinese medicine for thousands of years. With their anti-inflammatory, anti-viral, and detoxing properties, both turmeric and ginger are superfoods worth adding to your meals. Fresh roots are the best form, especially when making teas. When buying them ground as spices, it is worth spending a little bit more and getting the good quality, organic kinds.

2 tablespoons extra-virgin olive oil
1 yellow onion, thinly sliced
1 medium zucchini, spiralized
¾ cup shiitake mushrooms, sliced
1 teaspoon Healing Immune Blend (page 9)
2 cups vegetable broth

Spice it up!
¼ teaspoon red paprika

1. In a medium stockpot over medium heat, heat the oil.
2. Add the onion and sauté until translucent.
3. Add the zoodles, mushrooms, spice blend, and paprika (if using), and carefully toss to combine well.
4. Add the broth, then cover and cook for about 10 minutes, or until the zucchini is tender.
5. Serve warm.

* **Prep tip:** If you don't have a spiralizer, simply use a vegetable peeler to peel the zucchini in long strips. Once you spiralize or peel the zucchini, let it drain on a paper towel for about 10 minutes. This will help remove some of the water.

* **Ingredient tip:** You can add some red chili flakes to make this ramen soup spicy.

Per serving: Calories: 335; Fat: 28g; Protein: 5g; Carbohydrates: 20g; Fiber: 4g; Sodium: 321mg

BUTTER LETTUCE WITH SESAME DRESSING

DAIRY-FREE • GLUTEN-FREE • NUT-FREE • SOY-FREE • VEGAN

Prep time: 5 minutes

Yield: 2 servings as a main, 4 servings as a side

I love getting recipe inspirations when my husband and I travel or eat in restaurants. During a recent trip to France, we went to one Asian fusion place that is quite famous in the United States and Paris. I ordered a salad to start with: just simple butter lettuce with cucumbers. The flavors were magnificent! Savory but sweet, spicy but not too spicy. As soon as we arrived home, I knew I had to try to re-create the recipe. And that is how this recipe was born.

1 head butter lettuce, washed and patted dry

½ English cucumber, thinly sliced

Gochugaru Sesame Seed Dressing with EVOO (page 155)

1. In a large bowl, combine the lettuce leaves and cucumbers.
2. Pour the dressing over the salad to your taste and toss.

* **Storage tip:** Store leftover dressing in a glass jar in the refrigerator.

Per serving: Calories: 170; Fat: 15g; Protein: 2g; Carbohydrates: 8g; Fiber: 2g; Sodium: 102mg

TRADITIONAL GREEK SALAD

GLUTEN-FREE • NUT-FREE • SOY-FREE • VEGETARIAN
Prep time: 5 minutes
Yield: 4 servings

A healthy Mediterranean diet encompasses an abundance of vegetables, fish and seafood, good olive oil, wonderful fruits such as figs, and nuts and seeds. It is truly my favorite and so very healthy! I recommend serving this salad with my light and fresh Basic EVOO and Lemon Dressing, but you can use whatever you like.

1¼ cups cherry tomatoes, halved
½ English cucumber, chopped
¾ cup fresh parsley
⅓ cup Greek Kalamata olives
1 small yellow onion, thinly sliced
Basic EVOO and Lemon Dressing (page 154), optional

1. In a large bowl, combine the tomatoes, cucumber, parsley, olives, and onion. Stir to incorporate.
2. Serve with Basic EVOO and Lemon Dressing, if desired.

✳ **Serving tip:** Try adding some crumbled feta cheese on top.

✳ **Seasonal tip:** Enjoy this salad in the summer when tomatoes are in season.

✳ **Substitution tip:** You can replace the onion with scallions.

Per serving: Calories: 165; Fat: 15g; Protein: 1g; Carbohydrates: 7g; Fiber: 2g; Sodium: 363mg

GARBANZO BEAN SALAD

DAIRY-FREE • GLUTEN-FREE • NUT-FREE • SOY-FREE • VEGAN

Prep time: 5 minutes

Yield: 4 servings

Garbanzo beans, aka chickpeas, are a great source of plant-based protein and fiber, as well as essential vitamins and minerals such as calcium, iron, magnesium, and vitamin B_6. This is one of those pantry items that is great to keep on hand for a quick salad idea such as this one, for soups and stews (page 35), or to make a yummy spread such as Beet and Bean Hummus (page 71). Top this salad with Basic EVOO and Lemon Dressing (page 154).

2 (13-ounce) cans garbanzo beans, rinsed and drained

1½ cups cherry tomatoes, halved

1 large English cucumber, cubed

3 scallions, chopped (green and white parts)

¼ cup fresh parsley, roughly chopped

1. In a large bowl, combine the garbanzo beans, tomatoes, cucumber, scallions, and parsley. Stir to combine.
2. Toss with Basic EVOO and Lemon Dressing and serve.

* **Storage tip:** This salad can be stored in a glass container in the refrigerator for up to 2 days.

Per serving: Calories: 367; Fat: 18g; Protein: 12g; Carbohydrates: 41g; Fiber: 11g; Sodium: 391mg

ROASTED BEET SALAD

GLUTEN-FREE • SOY-FREE • VEGETARIAN
Prep time: 5 minutes • **Cook time:** 30 minutes
Yield: 4 servings

Beets. People either love them or hate them. I happen to adore beets, but that was not always the case. When I was in elementary school, my dad bought a juicer, and every day he juiced beets, carrots, and apples for us. I remember him telling me that beets are the healthiest vegetable there is, and how they are great for a strong immune system. Now, knowing what I know today, I would applaud my dad! Antioxidant-rich, detoxing, anti-viral, and anti-inflammatory, beets are a true superfood.

3 tablespoons extra-virgin olive oil, divided
2 tablespoons rice vinegar
¼ teaspoon Himalayan salt
4 medium beets, quartered
¼ cup pistachios, chopped
¼ cup goat cheese, crumbled

1. Preheat the oven to 400°F.
2. In a bowl, mix 2 tablespoons of olive oil with the rice vinegar and salt. Set aside.
3. Line a baking sheet with parchment paper. Toss the beets with the remaining tablespoon of olive oil and spread on the baking sheet.
4. Cover with another sheet of parchment paper and bake until the beets are tender, 25 to 30 minutes.
5. Let the beets cool and transfer them to a bowl.
6. Toss the beets in the olive oil dressing and transfer to a serving plate.
7. Add goat cheese and pistachios on top.

* **Serving tip:** Adding some fresh parsley or microgreens on top takes this wonderful salad to the next level.

* **Substitution tip:** Omit the cheese to make this salad vegan. You can also replace the rice vinegar with white wine vinegar.

* **Storage tip:** Beets store well in the refrigerator. After roasting them, let them cool, toss them in rice vinegar and olive oil, and store in a glass container.

Per serving: Calories: 188; Fat: 15g; Protein: 4g; Carbohydrates: 10g; Fiber: 3g; Sodium: 175mg

ARUGULA WATERMELON SALAD

GLUTEN-FREE • NUT-FREE • SOY-FREE • VEGETARIAN

Prep time: 5 minutes
Yield: 1 or 2 servings

With its powerful, peppery flavor, arugula does not need much doctoring up. A simple EVOO and Lemon Dressing (page 154) or the olive oil and balsamic vinegar used here is all you need to make an arugula-based salad perfectly delicious. But in this recipe we'll combine it with creamy goat cheese and avocado and transform it into a fresh and juicy salad by adding some watermelon.

4 cups arugula
2 tablespoons extra-virgin olive oil
½ cup watermelon, cubed
¼ cup goat cheese, crumbled
¼ avocado, sliced
⅛ teaspoon sea salt (optional)
1 tablespoon balsamic vinegar

1. In a bowl, toss the arugula and olive oil.
2. Add the watermelon, goat cheese, avocado, and salt (if using), and toss lightly.
3. Drizzle balsamic vinegar on top and serve immediately.

✳ **Substitution tip:** You can use feta instead of goat cheese. Strawberries can replace the watermelon, and if you run out of arugula, try baby spinach.

Per serving: Calories: 462; Fat: 41g; Protein: 10g; Carbohydrates: 17g; Fiber: 6g; Sodium: 158mg

COLD BEAN SALAD

GLUTEN-FREE • NUT-FREE • SOY-FREE • VEGAN

Prep time: 5 minutes

Yield: 2 servings

Beans are a wonderful source of plant-based protein, fiber, vitamins, minerals, and complex carbohydrates, making them a good choice for our healthy eating repertoire. Beans are filling and you don't need to eat large portions to feel satisfied. If you are vegan, adding ½ cup beans to your salads will add good protein to your meal.

1 can black beans, rinsed and drained
1 green pepper (Cubanelle), chopped
⅓ cup fresh parsley, chopped
1 scallion (green and white part), chopped
Juice of ½ lemon
1 tablespoon extra-virgin olive oil
¼ teaspoon Himalayan salt

1. In a bowl, combine the beans, pepper, parsley, and scallions, and stir to blend.
2. Add the lemon juice, oil, and salt, and lightly toss.

✳ **Substitution tip:** You can use any color peppers of your choice. Scallions can be replaced with chives or red onion.

Per serving: Calories: 250; Fat: 8g; Protein: 12g; Carbohydrates: 35g; Fiber: 13g; Sodium: 165mg

ROASTED RED PEPPER SALAD

GLUTEN-FREE • NUT-FREE • SOY-FREE • VEGAN
Prep time: 5 minutes • **Cook time:** 30 minutes
Yield: 3 servings

If you want a crowd pleaser, look no further! This salad can be added to almost any main dish; it pairs well with meats and is a perfect salad for barbecues. I usually make a big batch so that we can enjoy it the whole week. The process of making roasted red peppers may seem intimidating, but if you follow the steps below, you will see how easy it is.

6 long red peppers, washed and patted dry
2 tablespoons extra-virgin olive oil
1 tablespoon white wine vinegar
¼ teaspoon Himalayan salt, plus more
1 tablespoon fresh parsley, chopped, for garnishing

1. Turn on the broiler and let it preheat while you prepare the peppers.
2. Line a baking sheet with parchment paper and add the peppers in a single layer, skin-side up.
3. Broil the peppers on one side until the skin starts bubbling, about 5 minutes. Flip the peppers and broil on the other side.
4. Keep turning until all sides of the pepper are brown and the skin is lifted up. This should take 15 to 20 minutes, depending on your oven.
5. Take the peppers out of the oven and cover the baking sheet with a kitchen towel. Let rest 10 minutes.
6. Peel the skin off the peppers and lay them flat on a serving plate.
7. Drizzle with the oil, vinegar, and salt. Gently toss with clean hands so the dressing is evenly applied.
8. Sprinkle with a little salt and parsley.
9. Serve right away or refrigerate for about 15 minutes to cool further.

* **Substitution tip:** If you cannot find any long red peppers, you can use red bell peppers.

* **Prep tip:** If you have a grill, you can grill the peppers instead of broiling them; the taste is even better if you have a charcoal grill.

Per serving: Calories: 186; Fat: 10g; Protein: 3g; Carbohydrates: 21g; Fiber: 7g; Sodium: 118mg

AVOCADO CORN SALAD WITH TAHINI DRESSING

GLUTEN-FREE • NUT-FREE • SOY-FREE • VEGAN
Prep time: 5 minutes
Yield: 4 servings

This simple salad uses just two main ingredients, avocado and corn, but the tahini dressing gives it depth while keeping it light. This salad pairs wonderfully with grilled, grass-fed steak or chicken breast, or even as a taco topping for Vegan Tacos (page 111). Due to the delicate nature of avocado, once you prepare the salad, you'll need to enjoy it right away because the avocado will brown.

2 avocados, peeled, pitted, and cubed
½ cup corn (drained if canned)
Tahini Dressing (page 156)
Fresh parsley, for garnishing

1. In a bowl, combine the avocado and corn and toss gently.
2. Pour the dressing over the avocado and corn and toss lightly to coat.
3. Add some fresh parsley on top as garnish.

* **Serving tip:** I love serving this salad over arugula or kale for an even more nutrient-dense dish.

Per serving (includes dressing): Calories: 255; Fat: 21g; Protein: 5g; Carbohydrates: 18g; Fiber: 10g; Sodium: 48mg

KALE SALAD WITH ROASTED BUTTERNUT SQUASH

DAIRY-FREE · GLUTEN-FREE · NUT-FREE · SOY-FREE · VEGAN
Prep time: 5 minutes, plus 20 minutes to cool · **Cook time:** 30 minutes
Yield: 2 to 4 servings

Once colder months arrive, it's time to warm up our plates and that includes our salads. Our bodies naturally follow the seasons—in summer, we need to cool down, so we lean toward colder foods; in winter, our bodies crave heat, so we seek warmer comfort foods. Did you ever notice it's hard to eat a soup in the summer and cold smoothies do not go down as easily during the winter? That is precisely because of our natural seasonal body clock. Fall and winter are a great time to add roasted root veggies to our plates.

1 (16-ounce) package butternut squash, cubed
1 large shallot, thinly sliced
¼ teaspoon Himalayan salt
1 tablespoon extra-virgin olive oil
3 cups kale, washed, roughly chopped
Dijon Mustard Dressing (page 157)
¼ cup pumpkin seeds, roasted and unsalted

1. Preheat the oven to 400°F.
2. Line a baking sheet with parchment paper. Set aside.
3. In a bowl, combine the squash, shallots, salt, and olive oil and mix together to coat. Spread the squash in a single layer on the prepared baking sheet.
4. Roast until the squash is tender and looks golden, 25 to 30 minutes.
5. Cool to room temperature.
6. Put the kale in a large salad bowl and pour the dressing on top. Massage the kale until the kale absorbs the dressing and becomes soft.
7. Add the butternut squash to the kale, and sprinkle pumpkin seeds on top.

✳ **Ingredient tip:** Raw kale is very tough to chew unless you "massage" it with dressing. Simply wash your hands, mix the dressing, pour it over the kale, and squeeze it with your hands. The more you massage kale, the softer it will become.

Per serving: Calories: 385; Fat: 28g; Protein: 9g; Carbohydrates: 33g; Fiber: 7g; Sodium: 372mg

ARUGULA SALAD WITH BAKED ACORN SQUASH AND POMEGRANATE SEEDS

Prep time: 5 minutes
Yield: 2 to 3 servings

This salad showcases the fall season and everything that comes with it. Roasted squash, seasonal Brussels sprouts, pumpkin seeds, and pomegranate—fall in a bowl, wouldn't you say? Brussels sprouts are great sources of antioxidants as well as vitamin C, protein, and fiber. Rich in magnesium and iron, pumpkin seeds are a great source of plant-based protein and fiber, magnesium, iron, and essential fatty acids. Deliciously sweet pomegranate is high in antioxidants and immune-boosting vitamin C. Dress this salad with Basic EVOO and Lemon Dressing (page 154) or Tahini Dressing (page 156).

Extra-virgin olive oil, for coating squash
1 medium acorn squash, cut into rounds
4 cups arugula
½ cup Brussels sprouts, shaved or thinly sliced
⅓ cup pomegranate seeds
¼ cup pumpkin seeds

1. Preheat the oven to 400°F.
2. Line a baking sheet with parchment paper. Put the acorn squash on the baking sheet and gently toss with olive oil to coat. Spread in a single layer and bake for 20 to 25 minutes, until squash is tender.
3. Meanwhile, in a bowl, combine the arugula, Brussels sprouts, pomegranate, and pumpkin seeds and toss with the dressing of choice.
4. Add acorn squash on top and drizzle additional dressing on top.

✳ **Substitution tip:** You can use butternut squash in this recipe as well. You can also use unsalted sunflower seeds instead of pumpkin seeds.

Per serving: Calories: 351; Fat: 22g; Protein: 8g; Carbohydrates: 34g; Fiber: 7g; Sodium: 352mg

Classic Guacamole
page 59
with Gluten-Free
Biscuits with Pumpkin
and Sunflower Seeds
page 69

CHAPTER FOUR

SNACKS AND SMALL PLATES

This is the "fun chapter" of the cookbook because it contains everyone's favorite snack foods and some great crowd-pleasing dishes. From classic guacamole and baked chicken wings to homemade crackers and eggplant dip, there's a party for every taste bud. My Baked Tuna Melts will take you back to your childhood, while Beet and Bean Hummus will bring on an explosion of flavors in just one bite! Use this chapter as your go-to when you want to step up your snack game or when you need an array of fun appetizers and small bites. Have fun mixing and matching these recipes, and perhaps bring on one of the fun salads from the previous chapter as well!

Honey-Almond Greek Yogurt with Berries **57**

Raw Veggies with Yogurt Tzatziki **58**

✳ Classic Guacamole **59**

Tuna Lettuce Cups **60**

Baked Tuna Melts **61**

Baked Sweet Potato Fries with Spicy Yogurt Sauce **62**

Sweet Potato Toasts **64**

Baked Chicken Wings with Sriracha Glaze **65**

Stuffed Mushrooms with Spinach and Goat Cheese **66**

Broccoli Pizza Crust **67**

Flaxseed Sesame Protein Crackers **68**

✳ Gluten-Free Biscuits with Pumpkin and Sunflower Seeds 69

Beet and Bean Hummus 71

Cucumber Slices with Vegan Cream Cheese and Chives 72

Roasted Eggplant Dip 73

HONEY-ALMOND GREEK YOGURT WITH BERRIES

GLUTEN-FREE • SOY-FREE • VEGETARIAN

Prep time: 5 minutes

Yield: 1 serving

This recipe is the first in this chapter for a reason. My idea is to show you how easy it can be to make healthy snacks. Already-sweetened yogurts contain up to 4 teaspoons of sugar per serving. In some cases, they include high-fructose corn syrup, not even cane sugar. And yes, you guessed it: There is hardly any fruit in those yogurts. Making your own is a much healthier alternative.

1 (6-ounce) container plain Greek yogurt

1 tablespoon chopped roasted almonds

⅓ cup fresh berries

1 teaspoon raw honey

1. In a glass bowl, stir together the yogurt and almonds.
2. Add the berries and drizzle honey on top.

✳ **Ingredient tip:** Frozen berries can be used instead of fresh berries. Thaw them for 5 minutes and add them to the yogurt before the almonds.

Per serving: Calories: 188; Fat: 9g; Protein: 8g; Carbohydrates: 22g; Fiber: 2g; Sodium: 79mg

RAW VEGGIES WITH YOGURT TZATZIKI

GLUTEN-FREE • NUT-FREE • SOY-FREE • VEGETARIAN

Prep time: 10 minutes
Yield: 4 servings

Store-bought dips are usually loaded with artificial ingredients, saturated fats, and inflammatory oils. And all that comes with high calories and very little in the way of beneficial nutrients. This delicious tzatziki recipe comes together easily, and its versatility makes it work as both a dip and a dressing. It works especially well with thicker lettuces such as romaine or cabbage. I also like to add this sauce to my taco bowls instead of sour cream—yum!

1 (6-ounce) container Greek yogurt
1 garlic clove, crushed
1 teaspoon lemon juice
1 teaspoon extra-virgin olive oil
⅛ teaspoon Himalayan salt
1 teaspoon fresh dill

* Suggested raw vegetables:
Bell peppers, sliced
Carrots, cut into thick sticks
Cucumbers, cut into thick sticks

1. In a bowl, combine the yogurt, garlic, lemon juice, olive oil, and salt. Stir well until blended.
2. Add the dill, stir, and spoon into a serving bowl. Arrange the raw vegetables around the sides and serve immediately.

* **Substitution tip:** You can use any veggies you like. I suggest trying celery, snap peas, broccoli florets, French green beans, and endive.

Per serving: Calories: 39; Fat: 3g; Protein: 2g; Carbohydrates: 3g; Fiber: 0g; Sodium: 59mg

CLASSIC GUACAMOLE

DAIRY-FREE • GLUTEN-FREE • NUT-FREE • SOY-FREE • VEGAN

Prep time: 5 minutes
Yield: 2 to 4 servings

Avocado is a wonderful source of healthy omega fats and a good source of plant-based protein and fiber. With its dense nutritional profile, avocado is a superfood that certainly has a place in a clean eating lifestyle. However, some caution is needed when it comes to portion sizes, due to its high fat content. Typically, a quarter to a half of an avocado is a good amount to add to smoothies, or to top salads or toast. Of course, depending what the rest of your day looks like in terms of fat intake, a big bowl of guacamole might be just right.

2 avocados, peeled, pitted, and mashed
¼ teaspoon Himalayan salt
Juice of ½ lemon
¼ cup cherry tomatoes, diced small
½ shallot, minced
1 tablespoon fresh cilantro, chopped

1. In a bowl, combine the avocado, salt, and lemon juice. Mix well.
2. Add the tomatoes and shallots, and gently stir to combine.
3. Top with the cilantro.
4. Serve with some organic baked corn chips, celery, endive, or romaine lettuce.

* **Prep tip:** If you wish to make this ahead of time, save the pit and put it inside the guacamole. When stored this way in the refrigerator, it will help prevent browning.

* **Serving tip:** You can add some red chili flakes on top, if you like your guac spicy.

* **Substitution tip:** Try lime instead of lemon. Parsley can also be used instead of cilantro.

Per serving: Calories: 373; Fat: 31g; Protein: 7g; Carbohydrates: 26g; Fiber: 17g; Sodium: 163mg

TUNA LETTUCE CUPS

DAIRY-FREE • GLUTEN-FREE • SOY-FREE • NUT-FREE

Prep time: 10 minutes

Yield: 2 to 4 servings

Tuna lettuce cups are one of my favorite low-carbohydrate lunch or snack ideas. They are easy to make, and if you do some prep ahead of time, they become even easier. Tuna stores well in the refrigerator, so if you make a big batch of this tuna, you can store it in a covered glass container for about 3 days and it will still be fresh. You can also wash the lettuce, pat it dry, and wrap it in a paper towel. Lettuce stays fresh like this for days! When you're ready for your lunch or snack, this tasty meal comes together in a snap.

2 tablespoons extra-virgin olive oil

1 tablespoon whole-grain mustard

¼ teaspoon Himalayan salt

2 (5-ounce) cans skipjack tuna in water, drained

1 tablespoon chives, chopped

¼ cup carrots, shredded

8 romaine or butter lettuce leaves, washed and dried

1. In a bowl, whisk together the olive oil, mustard, and salt and set aside.
2. In a separate bowl, combine the tuna, chives, and carrots and stir well.
3. Pour the dressing on the tuna mixture and gently toss to combine.
4. Take one leaf of lettuce and spoon some tuna on it. Repeat until you've used all the tuna and lettuce leaves.

* **Serving tip:** Feel free to garnish this salad with fresh parsley and black pepper.

* **Substitution tip:** Make this your own. You can use albacore tuna instead of skipjack. You can use Dijon mustard instead of whole-grain mustard. If you are looking to add even more fiber to this dish, try endive instead of the romaine; you'll just need more endive because the leaves are smaller. Celery can also replace the carrots, and you can use scallions instead of chives.

Per serving: Calories: 247; Fat: 15g; Protein: 24g; Carbohydrates: 6g; Fiber: 3g; Sodium: 342mg

BAKED TUNA MELTS

DAIRY-FREE • NUT-FREE • SOY-FREE

Prep time: 5 minutes • **Cook time:** 10 minutes
Yield: 2 servings

Growing up, I used to love toast sandwiches. We made them with white bread, sour cream or mayo, ham, shredded cheese, and ketchup. Because these aren't as popular in the United States as they are in Europe, I stopped eating them and essentially forgot about them. If I were to make one today, I would select a healthier version that looked something like this: whole-grain bread, Dijon mustard and vegan mayo, smoked turkey breast, and shredded vegan cheese or shredded organic mozzarella. My love for finding healthier alternatives led me to develop this recipe where I use tuna as the main ingredient in the toast sandwich.

1 (5-ounce) can skipjack tuna, in water, drained
⅛ teaspoon Himalayan salt
1 tablespoon vegan or olive-oil mayonnaise
1 tablespoon Dijon mustard
2 slices whole-grain bread
2 tablespoons vegan or regular shredded mozzarella

1. Preheat the oven to 400°F.
2. In a bowl, mix together the tuna and salt.
3. Add the mayo and Dijon and mix.
4. Split the tuna mixture in half and spread it on the 2 slices of bread.
5. Add 1 tablespoon of cheese to each of the melts.
6. Place the bread directly on the center rack of the oven.
7. Bake for about 10 minutes, or until the cheese melts.

* **Serving tip:** Adding 1 tablespoon of chopped onions, chives, or scallions makes these melted toasts even richer in taste. I also love topping these with fresh herbs and black pepper.

* **Substitution tip:** Most types of bread work here—I even love this on high-fiber crackers.

Per serving: Calories: 167; Fat: 6g; Protein: 17g; Carbohydrates: 12g; Fiber: 2g; Sodium: 356mg

BAKED SWEET POTATO FRIES WITH SPICY YOGURT SAUCE

GLUTEN-FREE • NUT-FREE • SOY-FREE • VEGAN
Prep time: 5 minutes · **Cook time:** 20 minutes
Yield: 3 servings

I love French fries and especially sweet potato fries. Unfortunately, most frozen French fries are made with cheap oils (peanut, soy, corn), and they contain unnecessary ingredients such as starches and gums. Our bodies have a natural desire for sweets, so adding sweet vegetables to your diet helps satisfy that need. Sweet potatoes, butternut squash, carrots, and beets can all help manage sugar cravings and prevent late-night sweet-tooth attacks. As a bonus, sweet potatoes are a great source of fiber as well as of vitamins A, C, and B_6.

FOR THE SPICY YOGURT SAUCE

1 (6-ounce) container Greek yogurt
1 to 2 tablespoons sriracha

FOR THE SWEET POTATOES

2 medium sweet potatoes, washed and dried
½ teaspoon Himalayan salt
⅛ cup extra-virgin olive oil

Spice it up!

1 teaspoon chili powder
½ teaspoon garlic powder

1. Preheat the oven to 425°F.
2. **To make the spicy yogurt sauce:** Mix the yogurt and sriracha and set aside.
3. **To make the sweet potatoes:** Cut the sweet potatoes into equal ½-inch wedges and put them in a bowl.
4. Mix the salt with the chili powder and garlic powder (if using).
5. Sprinkle the spices and olive oil over the potatoes. Mix well to coat.

6. Roast the potatoes for about 15 minutes on one side, then flip over and cook for another 5 minutes.
7. Cool the sweet potatoes on a wire rack for about 5 minutes. Serve with spicy yogurt sauce for dipping.

* **Prep tip:** I like baking a big batch of sweet potatoes and storing them in a glass container in the refrigerator. Over the next 2 days, I use them cold as a salad topping.

* **Substitution tip:** You can use any type of hot sauce instead of sriracha. Because hot sauce is much spicier, start with 1 teaspoon of hot sauce and adjust up to your liking.

Per serving: Calories: 192; Fat: 11g; Protein: 3g; Carbohydrates: 20g; Fiber: 3g; Sodium: 298mg

SWEET POTATO TOASTS

GLUTEN-FREE • NUT-FREE • SOY-FREE • VEGAN
Prep time: 5 minutes • **Cook time:** 20 minutes
Yield: 2 servings

This dish makes a great snack or side (see the Serving tip for a yummy topping idea). I often like adding fun sides like this when making something simple such as grilled chicken or baked codfish. Because sweet potatoes are a starchy vegetable, we don't need to add any grains to our meal—this will fill us up. Baked chicken and one serving of sweet potato toast with a nice green salad on the side makes a colorful and nutrient-dense dinner. For lunch, these toasts pair great with some arugula or romaine hearts with Basic EVOO and Lemon Dressing (page 154).

1 large sweet potato, cut into ¼- to ½-inch slices lengthwise
1 teaspoon Taco Seasoning (page 9)
1 tablespoon extra-virgin olive oil
¼ teaspoon Himalayan salt (optional)

1. Preheat the oven to 400°F.
2. Line a baking sheet with parchment paper. Put the potatoes on the baking sheet. Sprinkle the taco spice on each of the slices, then rub all the slices with olive oil.
3. Bake for 15 to 20 minutes, or until cooked.
4. Serve warm.

* **Serving tip:** For a wonderful topping, mix ½ cup of rinsed black beans and ¼ cup of salsa. Top each toast with some mashed avocado, then the bean salsa mixture. Add fresh parsley or cilantro if desired.

Per serving: Calories: 116; Fat: 7g; Protein: 1g; Carbohydrates: 13g; Fiber: 2g; Sodium: 58mg

BAKED CHICKEN WINGS WITH SRIRACHA GLAZE

DAIRY-FREE · GLUTEN-FREE · NUT-FREE · SOY-FREE
Prep time: 5 minutes · **Cook time:** 40 minutes
Yield: 12 wings

This is a favorite crowd-pleasing food to make for big parties. Typically, wings are deep-fried, and restaurants often add white flour to the batter. Baking them in the oven is healthier, and they are just as delicious—crispy on the outside and juicy on the inside. You can also omit the glaze and just bake the wings until crispy.

FOR THE GLAZE

¼ cup sriracha
1 tablespoon mirin (sweet Japanese cooking wine; see substitution tip)
2 teaspoons raw honey

FOR THE CHICKEN WINGS

12 chicken wings, washed and patted dry
½ teaspoon Himalayan salt
2 tablespoons extra-virgin olive oil

Spice it up!

1 teaspoon garlic powder

1. Preheat the oven to 400°F. Line a baking sheet with parchment paper and set aside.
2. **To make the glaze:** In a small bowl, mix together the sriracha, mirin, and honey. Whisk and set aside.
3. **To make the chicken wings:** In a medium bowl, combine the wings, salt, olive oil, and garlic powder (if using). Toss until the wings are evenly coated.
4. Lay out the wings on the prepared baking sheet.
5. Bake the wings for 25 minutes. Take them out, glaze them, and bake for another 5 minutes. Repeat 3 times. You can put the wings on broil for the last 3 minutes, if you like them well done.
6. Cool the wings on a cooking rack to stay crisp.

* **Serving tip:** Serve these with Spicy Yogurt Sauce (page 62) or your favorite dipping sauce.

* **Substitution tip:** You can use white wine or rice vinegar instead of mirin.

Per serving (4 wings): Calories: 386; Fat: 29g; Protein: 27g; Carbohydrates: 4g; Fiber: 0g; Sodium: 398mg

STUFFED MUSHROOMS WITH SPINACH AND GOAT CHEESE

GLUTEN-FREE • SOY-FREE • NUT-FREE

Prep time: 5 minutes • **Cook time:** 20 minutes

Yield: 4 servings

Mushrooms are an excellent source of plant-based protein, fiber, B vitamins, potassium, and vitamin D, and they're rich in antioxidants. Why are antioxidants important? They help lessen oxidative stress, which can contribute to aging and many chronic diseases. In short, antioxidants help us fight the bad guys and stay healthy. All that said, these stuffed mushrooms are decadent and restaurant-worthy!

1 (8-ounce) package baby bella mushrooms

2 tablespoons extra-virgin olive oil, divided

4 cups baby spinach

1 large garlic clove, minced

¼ teaspoon Himalayan salt

4 tablespoons goat cheese

1. Preheat the oven to 400°F.
2. Peel the mushrooms, remove the stem, and set them aside. Put the mushroom caps in a bowl.
3. Drizzle 1 tablespoon of oil over the mushroom caps, then toss. Arrange the mushrooms in a baking dish and set aside.
4. In a small, nonstick sauté pan or skillet, heat the remaining tablespoon of oil.
5. Add the spinach and sauté for 1 or 2 minutes. Add the garlic and salt, stir to combine, and wilt the spinach, another 1 or 2 minutes.
6. Put some of the spinach mixture inside the cap of each mushroom. Sprinkle wiith goat cheese.
7. Bake until the mushrooms are tender and the cheese becomes soft, 15 to 20 minutes.
8. Serve immediately.

✳ **Ingredient tip:** Save the stems and chop them up for use in omelets.

✳ **Substitution tip:** You can use portabella mushrooms for this recipe as well. Because they are bigger, you'll need to double the recipe for the spinach depending on how many you are making.

Per serving: Calories: 99; Fat: 9g; Protein: 3g; Carbohydrates: 4g; Fiber: 1g; Sodium: 139mg

BROCCOLI PIZZA CRUST

DAIRY-FREE • GLUTEN-FREE • NUT-FREE • SOY-FREE • VEGAN
Prep time: 5 minutes • **Cook time:** 40 minutes
Yield: 3 servings

I love finding ways to transform my favorite dishes into healthier and more nutritious versions so that I can enjoy them more often. Here, I've created a delcious, high-protein pizza crust recipe. This recipe makes 3 individual-size pizzas. If not using all three, freeze them in between parchment paper. When ready to cook, add toppings of choice and bake at 425°F until the cheese is bubbly.

Olive oil, for greasing the pan
3 cups broccoli, riced (see Ingredient tip)
1½ cups egg whites
1½ cups almond flour
1 teaspoon baking powder
½ teaspoon Himalayan salt

Spice it up!
¼ teaspoon garlic powder
½ teaspoon oregano

1. Preheat the oven to 400°F. Grease a baking sheet with baking soda and set aside.
2. In a large bowl, combine the broccoli, egg whites, almond flour, baking powder, salt, and garlic powder and oregano (if using), and stir to combine.
3. Divide the mixture into thirds and form pizzas on the prepared baking sheet. The mixture will be wet, but it will dry as it cooks.
4. Bake for 30 minutes without opening the oven. After 30 minutes, take pizzas out, flip them over, and bake for another 10 minutes.
5. Add your favorite pizza toppings, such as tomato sauce, shredded mozzarella, and mushrooms, and set the pizzas back in the oven until cheese is bubbly, about 5 minutes.

* **Ingredient tip:** Grocery stores often carry riced broccoli in both fresh and frozen varieties. You can use a food processor to pulse broccoli florets or a grater to make riced broccoli.

* **Prep tip:** For a crispy crust, broil or convection-bake the second side, being careful not to burn if broiling—watch it closely.

Per serving: Calories: 383; Fat: 26g; Protein: 26g; Carbohydrates: 18g; Fiber: 8g; Sodium: 547mg

FLAXSEED SESAME PROTEIN CRACKERS

GLUTEN-FREE • NUT-FREE • SOY-FREE • VEGAN
Prep time: 5 minutes • **Cook time:** 30 minutes
Yield: About 12 crackers

Store-bought crackers are highly processed and most of those sold in ordinary supermarkets contain less-than-optimal ingredients. Some food companies use the cheapest oils, such as peanut or soy, high-fructose corn syrup to sweeten, and additives and other artificial ingredients that are not great for our gut health and digestion. These crackers are easy to make and so delicious, every member of the family will enjoy them.

2 cups spelt flour
1 cup flax seeds
1 cup sesame seeds
1 cup water
¼ cup extra-virgin olive oil
1 teaspoon Himalayan salt

1. Preheat the oven to 375°F. Line a baking sheet with parchment paper and set aside.
2. In a bowl, mix the flour with the seeds, then add the water, oil, and salt. Stir until you get a thick dough-texture mixture.
3. On a clean, lightly floured surface, use a rolling pin to roll out the dough to about ¼-inch thickness.
4. Using a small coffee cup, cut out crackers and put them on the prepared baking sheet.
5. Bake until crispy, about 20 minutes.
6. Let the crackers cool on a cooling rack before storing them in a glass container at room temperature.

✳ **Substitution tip:** Get creative with the seeds you use! I also tried these with pumpkin seeds and they came out delicious.

Per serving (1 cracker): Calories: 266; Fat: 18g; Protein: 8g; Carbohydrates: 21g; Fiber: 7g; Sodium: 107mg

GLUTEN-FREE BISCUITS WITH PUMPKIN AND SUNFLOWER SEEDS

GLUTEN-FREE • NUT-FREE • SOY-FREE • VEGAN
Prep time: 5 minutes • **Cook time:** 20 minutes
Yield: 12 biscuits

These high-protein biscuits are a crowd pleaser. Why not surprise your family at the next weekend brunch and replace boring white bread rolls with these delicious high-protein biscuits? I can promise you that no one will complain. These biscuits are also great to have for breakfast with some creamy eggs on the side, or with vegan or regular cream cheese and some fresh tomatoes. These are best if you make them on the day that you're serving them—that way, they will be crispy on the outside and soft on the inside. You can enjoy them the next day as well, but the texture will be softer; similar to corn bread.

2 cups almond flour
¼ cup ground flaxseed
¼ cup sunflower seeds
¼ cup pumpkin seeds
¼ cup extra-virgin olive oil
1 teaspoon baking soda
1 teaspoon baking powder
¼ teaspoon Himalayan salt
1 cup room-temperature water

Spice it up!
¼ teaspoon brown sugar

1. Preheat the oven to 375°F if you have a convection oven, or 400°F if you have a conventional oven.
2. In a large bowl, combine the almond flour, flaxseed, sunflower seeds, pumpkin seeds, olive oil, baking soda, baking powder, salt, and brown sugar (if using).
3. Add the water slowly and stir just to combine. The batter will be thick and sticky.
4. Cover with plastic wrap and refrigerate for at least 30 minutes.

Continued ❯

Continued

5. Line a baking sheet with parchment paper. Using an ice cream scoop, scoop the batter into 12 biscuits onto the prepared baking sheet.
6. If you have a convection oven, bake for about 20 minutes, then switch to 400°F and convection-bake for the last 10 minutes. If you have a conventional oven, bake for about 25 minutes, until a toothpick inserted in a biscuit comes out clean.

✳ **Storage tip:** To store overnight, use a covered glass container. If you see a little greening on day 2, it's not mold—this is due to the sunflower seeds and baking soda reacting together.

Per serving (1 biscuit): Calories: 175; Fat: 16g; Protein: 5g; Carbohydrates: 5g; Fiber: 3g; Sodium: 163mg

BEET AND BEAN HUMMUS

GLUTEN-FREE • NUT-FREE • SOY-FREE • VEGAN

Prep time: 5 minutes

Yield: About 2 cups

Hummus is such a great snack when you need something quick, nutritious, and filling. I started making my own hummus a long time ago, but the idea of adding beets came about when I was studying nutrition. I've read so many articles that tout beets as superstar vegetables—so I started juicing them, adding them to my salads and morning smoothies, even baking sweets with them. And that's how I started adding beets to hummus, too. Guess what? I never looked back and don't even make regular hummus anymore. It's that delicious.

1 (13-ounce) can cannellini beans, rinsed and drained

1 medium beet, peeled, cooked, and roughly chopped

1 large garlic clove

2 tablespoons tahini

2 tablespoons extra-virgin olive oil

¼ teaspoon Himalayan salt

1. In a food processor or high-speed blender, combine the beans, beets, garlic, tahini, olive oil, and salt.
2. Blend until smooth.
3. Enjoy on sourdough toast or your favorite crackers, or with some celery.

* **Storage tip:** You can store hummus in a glass container in the refrigerator for up to 1 week.

* **Substitution tip:** Try white beans instead of cannellini beans.

Per serving (¼ cup): Calories: 107; Fat: 6g; Protein: 4g; Carbohydrates: 11g; Fiber: 3g; Sodium: 52mg

CUCUMBER SLICES WITH VEGAN CREAM CHEESE AND CHIVES

GLUTEN-FREE • SOY-FREE • VEGAN

Prep time: 10 min
Yield: ¾ to 1 cup cream cheese

This delicious non-dairy cream cheese is so versatile. I love having it with fresh tomatoes and parsley, with prosciutto or smoked salmon, or with creamy eggs. It's not hard to make, but it takes a little bit of patience during the blending process. I promise it is so worth it! You may need to open the blender a few times and push down the cashews, but other than that, just wait for it to blend down nicely into a creamy paste.

1⅛ cups cashews, unsalted
Juice of ½ lemon
¼ teaspoon Himalayan salt, or more
2 tablespoons fresh chives, plus more for garnish
1 long English cucumber, cut into thick rounds

1. Soak the cashews in water overnight.
2. Drain and reserve ¼ cup of the liquid.
3. Put the cashews in a high-speed blender or food processor and start blending on low. Slowly increase the speed.
4. When cashews become paste (about 5 minutes), add the lemon juice and salt. Blend for another 2 minutes.
5. Scoop the cream cheese into a bowl. Add the chives and stir to combine.
6. Arrange cucumber slices on a plate and top each with about 1 teaspoon of cream cheese.
7. Transfer the leftover cream cheese to a glass container, and store in the refrigerator for up to 1 week.

* **Serving tip:** Add more fresh chives on top, as well as freshly ground pepper, if desired.

* **Substitution tip:** Omit the chives and make the cream cheese plain. Tastes just as good.

* **Prep tip:** I usually leave the cashews in the water for just one night, but you can do it for two; just put them in the refrigerator the second day. Keeping them in the water longer will soften the cashews even more and the cream cheese will be creamier.

Per serving (2 tablespoons): Calories: 164; Fat: 12g; Protein: 5g; Carbohydrates: 11g; Fiber: 1g; Sodium: 56mg

ROASTED EGGPLANT DIP

GLUTEN-FREE • NUT-FREE • SOY-FREE • VEGAN

Prep time: 5 minutes • **Cook time:** 25 minutes

Yield: 1 to 2 cups (depending on size of eggplant)

Before moving to the United States, I had never tasted anything but typical Serbian food. I didn't know what tacos were, or tabbouleh, or dumplings. One of my first best friends was an amazing cook and most of her dishes had Middle Eastern influences. She taught me how to make traditional hummus and introduced me to tahini—what a revelation! I had no idea such a thing existed, nor had I ever experienced such complex flavor. Today, I love being inspired by different cultures and combining those discoveries with what I grew up on—like this delicious eggplant dip.

2 tablespoons extra-virgin olive oil, divided

1 large eggplant, cut lengthwise

2 small garlic cloves, crushed

1 tablespoon tahini

1 teaspoon lemon juice

¼ teaspoon Himalayan salt

1. Preheat the oven to 425°F. Line a baking sheet with parchment paper and set aside.
2. Rub 1 tablespoon of olive oil on both insides of the eggplant.
3. Put the eggplant, cut-side down, on the prepared baking sheet and roast until soft, about 25 minutes.
4. While the eggplant is still hot, use a fork to scrape out the meaty part into a glass bowl.
5. Add the crushed garlic, tahini, remaining tablespoon of olive oil, lemon, and salt. Mix well.
6. Serve immediately.

∗ **Serving tip:** Garnish with some fresh parsley, if desired. Serve with warm corn tortillas, warm pita bread wedges, or organic corn chips. For a lighter version, serve with endive or romaine lettuce leaves.

∗ **Storage tip:** You can double the recipe and, after the dip cools down, store it in the refrigerator in a covered glass container. It's just as delicious cold.

Per serving (¼ cup): Calories: 59; Fat: 4g; Protein: 1g; Carbohydrates: 5g; Fiber: 2g; Sodium: 42mg

Greek-Style Quinoa Salad
page 77

CHAPTER FIVE

RICE, GRAINS, AND BEANS

Versatile, economical, and filling, this category of foods can be taken in countless directions. This chapter contains a variety of stand-alone dishes, such as Quinoa Bowl with Roasted Broccoli and Asparagus, and String Bean Casserole with Chicken, as well as some side dishes such as Vegetable Fried Rice, and Baked Beans in Tomato Sauce. Legume- and bean-based soups in this chapter make great additions to any salad from chapter 3 or starters to any of the main dishes from chapters 7 and 8. The recipes in this chapter are inspired by many different cuisines, such as Mediterranean, East Asian, Italian, and Mexican. I also included some Serbian recipes that I used to eat as a child, and they are still my favorites to this day.

* Greek-Style Quinoa Salad **77**

Lemony Asparagus Risotto **78**

Vegetable Fried Rice **80**

Swiss Chard Rolls with Rice in Tomato Sauce **81**

Tri-Colored Pepper Medley with Brown Rice **83**

Pea Stew with Chicken **85**

String Bean Casserole with Chicken **87**

Baked Beans in Tomato Sauce **88**

Beans with Baby Spinach **89**

Adzuki Bean Soup **90**

Green Lentil Stew **91**

Lentil Bisque 92

Green Lentil Salad with Dijon Mustard Dressing 93

Spicy Shrimp Pasta Arrabbiata 94

Creamy Chicken and Broccoli Pasta 96

GREEK-STYLE QUINOA SALAD

GLUTEN-FREE • NUT-FREE • SOY-FREE • VEGAN

Prep time: 5 minutes • **Cook time:** 25 minutes

Yield: 4 to 6 servings

This is the first meal I ever made with quinoa. I was hesitant to try it, but I figured if I added it to something I already loved, it wouldn't be that bad. It was love at first bite! Quinoa is a complete protein, so if you make, say, roasted veggies, you can add quinoa and not need additional animal-based protein. I also sprinkle cooked quinoa on any salad I make, to add protein and some crunch.

FOR THE DRESSING

¼ cup extra-virgin olive oil

Juice of ½ large lemon

½ teaspoon Himalayan salt

FOR THE QUINOA

2 cups quinoa

1¼ cups cherry tomatoes, quartered

½ English cucumber, cubed

½ cup Kalamata olives, chopped

1. **For the dressing:** In a bowl, whisk together the oil, lemon juice, and salt and set aside.
2. **For the quinoa:** Rinse the quinoa until the water runs clear.
3. In a medium saucepan, bring 4 cups of water to a boil.
4. Add the quinoa, cover, and simmer on low for about 20 minutes.
5. Open the pot, fluff the quinoa with a fork, cover, and let it rest for about 5 minutes.
6. Transfer the quinoa to a large wooden or glass salad bowl and allow it to cool.
7. Once the quinoa cools to room temperature, add the tomatoes, cucumbers, and olives. Stir to combine.
8. Add the dressing and toss.

* **Serving tip:** If you love fresh herbs, add ¾ cup fresh parsley to this salad. Scallions or sliced red onion is also a great addition, if you like more intense flavor.

* **Storage tip:** Once dressed, this salad stores well for about 2 days in the refrigerator. Plain cooked quinoa will last for a full week in the refrigerator.

Per serving (6): Calories: 311; Fat: 14g; Protein: 9g; Carbohydrates: 39g; Fiber: 5g; Sodium: 184mg

LEMONY ASPARAGUS RISOTTO

GLUTEN-FREE • NUT-FREE • SOY-FREE • VEGETARIAN

Prep time: 5 minutes • **Cook time:** 20 minutes

Yield: 2 servings

Arborio rice is a short-grain rice typically used for risotto. The texture is similar to sushi rice, yet with the chewiness of brown rice. This simple recipe comes together quickly and the lemon ties together the asparagus and Parmesan cheese. This is a great spring and summer dish, and it's also lovely served with butter lettuce and scallions, along with my Basic EVOO and Lemon Dressing (page 154).

1 tablespoon extra-virgin olive oil

1 yellow onion, chopped

¾ cup asparagus, woody ends trimmed and cut into 1-inch pieces

Juice of ½ lemon

1 cup Arborio rice, washed and drained

½ teaspoon Himalayan salt

2 cups water

2 tablespoons freshly grated Parmesan cheese

Spice it up!

1 teaspoon Mediterranean Blend (page 9)

Freshly ground black pepper

1. In a medium saucepan over medium heat, heat the olive oil.
2. Add the onions and sauté until translucent, then add the asparagus and lemon juice. Stir and cook for about 1 minute.
3. Add the rice, salt, spice blend (if using), and water. Cover tightly, reduce heat to low, and cook for about 20 minutes.
4. Stir in the Parmesan cheese, and cook for 1 to 2 minutes. Add freshly ground pepper, if desired.
5. Serve warm.

✳ **Prep tip:** If you love garlic, I recommend adding 1 clove of minced garlic along with the onions.

✳ **Substitution tip:** You can swap the Parmesan for Pecorino Romano or vegan Parmesan.

Per serving: Calories: 473; Fat: 9g; Protein: 10g; Carbohydrates: 88g; Fiber: 5g; Sodium: 467mg

VEGETABLE FRIED RICE

GLUTEN-FREE • NUT-FREE • SOY-FREE • VEGETARIAN

Prep time: 5 minutes • **Cook time:** 25 minutes
Yield: 4 servings

White rice is not the enemy. White pasta is not the enemy. It's the quantities we consume that can become a problem. In restaurants, when you order vegetable fried rice or any pasta dish, you'll get an amount that's made for two people. And most of us finish the entire bowl anyway. These large portions make us overeat, and yep, we conclude, "Carbs are bad." Enjoy carbs. Portion control and balance are key.

2 cups water
1½ cups sushi rice
2 cups mixed frozen vegetables
3 tablespoons extra-virgin olive oil
1 yellow onion, chopped
1¼ teaspoons Himalayan salt

Spice it up!
1 teaspoon garlic powder

1. Pour the water into a medium stockpot and bring it to a boil. Add the rice, cover, and cook for about 20 minutes. Most of the liquid will evaporate.
2. Meanwhile, cook or steam the frozen vegetables (see Ingredient tip). Drain and set aside.
3. In a large, non-metal or cast-iron pan over medium heat, heat the oil and onion. After 1 minute, add the rice. Stir well to incorporate with the onion and make sure it doesn't stick to the pan.
4. Add the vegetables, garlic powder (if using), and salt. Stir and sauté another 2 minutes. The rice will start to brown on the bottom—that is okay. Scrape up the browned parts from the bottom and turn off the heat.

* **Prep tip:** If you have time, cook the rice the day before. It's easier to work with the next day, because it's drier and less sticky. Simply pick up the recipe at step 3.

* **Ingredient tip:** The easiest way to cook frozen vegetables is to add them to some hot water and boil for about 10 minutes, until tender.

Per serving: Calories: 428; Fat: 11g; Protein: 8g; Carbohydrates: 74g; Fiber: 7g; Sodium: 539mg

SWISS CHARD ROLLS WITH RICE IN TOMATO SAUCE

Prep time: 5 minutes • **Cook time:** 40 minutes

Yield: 2 to 4 servings

I always liked ordering this dish in restaurants that serve European food, but I never attempted to make it. My mother-in-law always mentioned how delicious it is and easy it is to make. Finally, I decided it was time to give it a shot, so we made it together one day. Her recipe included simple, real ingredients—nothing processed, just the way I like it. Clean and perfect! I believe you'll love this recipe—it's delicate, yet full of flavor.

¾ cup water

½ cup uncooked white rice

2 tablespoons extra-virgin olive oil, divided

1 medium carrot, finely grated

1 medium potato, finely grated

¾ teaspoon Himalayan salt, divided

¼ teaspoon freshly ground black pepper, plus more if desired

8 Swiss chard leaves, tough parts trimmed

¾ cup tomato puree

Spice it up!

½ teaspoon dried onion flakes

1. In a small saucepan, bring ¾ cup water to a boil. Add the rice, cover, and cook for about 12 minutes or until most of the water evaporates.
2. Meanwhile, in a small, nonstick sauté pan or skillet, heat the olive oil over medium heat and add the onion flakes (if using), the carrots, and the potatoes. Sauté for 1 to 2 minutes, then add ½ teaspoon of salt and the pepper.
3. Add the vegetable mixture to the rice, stir, and let it cool down for a few minutes.
4. Meanwhile, boil 2 cups of water with the remaining ¼ teaspoon salt. Turn off the heat. Using long kitchen tongs, dip a Swiss chard leaf in the water. Keep the leaf submerged for a few seconds to blanch the chard. Take it out and lay it flat on a plate. Repeat with the remaining greens. Reserve 2 cups of the water.

Continued ❯

Continued

5. Add the remaining tablespoon of olive oil to a medium saucepan and set aside. Take a Swiss chard leaf in the palm of your hand, with the inside of the leaf facing you, and place about 1½ tablespoons of the rice and vegetable mixture in the center. One by one, fold in the sides, forming a burrito-like roll. Place the rolls side by side in the oiled saucepan.
6. Once you are done making all 8 rolls, add the 2 cups of reserved liquid from blanching to the saucepan. Cover and cook on medium-low for about 15 minutes.
7. Add the tomato puree, the remaining ¼ teaspoon of salt, and some black pepper if desired. Cover and let simmer on low for another 25 minutes. Do not stir; just shake the pot gently to mix.

* **Prep tip:** Although this may seem like a complicated recipe because of its length, I can promise you it's not. Once you read through the steps, you'll realize how simple it is.

* **Serving tip:** Adding 1 to 2 tablespoons of Greek yogurt on top is a delicious way to serve this. Alternatively, unsweetened cashew yogurt also works well.

* **Substitution tip:** You can use freshly diced onion instead of dried onion flakes.

Per serving: Calories: 459; Fat: 15g; Protein: 11g; Carbohydrates: 75g; Fiber: 9g; Sodium: 640mg

TRI-COLORED PEPPER MEDLEY WITH BROWN RICE

GLUTEN-FREE • SOY-FREE • NUT-FREE
Prep time: 5 minutes • **Cook time:** 25 minutes
Yield: 3 servings

Traditionally called *Satarš* in Serbia, and very popular throughout southeast Europe, this pepper medley is delicious. It's typically served over mashed potatoes with meat on the side, but I also find it delicious as a vegetarian dish served simply over rice. This recipe makes a great quick weeknight dinner when you need something nutritious but are too tired to make anything elaborate. I often make a big batch of this dish on a Sunday and enjoy it over the next 5 days. It stores in the refrigerator well and reheats nicely.

3 cups water, divided
1 cup brown rice
2 tablespoons extra-virgin olive oil
1 yellow onion, chopped
5 bell peppers (green, yellow, red), sliced
1 teaspoon Himalayan salt
1 (13-ounce) can whole peeled tomatoes, in liquid, chopped
1 large egg, beaten

Spice it up!
¼ teaspoon cumin
½ teaspoon basil
Freshly ground black pepper

1. Bring 2¼ cups of water to a boil, then add the cumin (if using), and the rice. Cover, reduce heat to a simmer, and cook for about 25 minutes.
2. Meanwhile, in a sauté pan or skillet over medium heat, heat the olive oil. Add the onions and sauté about 1 minute. Add the peppers, salt, and basil (if using), then stir, cover, and let it simmer for another 2 minutes.
3. Add the tomatoes and the remaining ¾ cup of water, then cover and simmer for about 20 minutes.
4. Uncover, stir in the beaten egg, cover, and turn off the heat. Let it rest for about 2 minutes.
5. Serve the rice topped with the pepper medley. Sprinkle with black pepper if desired.

Continued ❯

Continued

* **Serving tip:** Enjoy this topped with fresh parsley.

* **Ingredient tip:** You can make this dish vegan by omitting the egg.

* **Substitution tip:** You can use any color peppers. I like using at least 2 different colors, as it's always nice to have that rainbow effect on the plate.

Per serving: Calories: 407; Fat: 13g; Protein: 10g; Carbohydrates: 65g; Fiber: 9g; Sodium: 575mg

PEA STEW WITH CHICKEN

GLUTEN-FREE • NUT-FREE • SOY-FREE • DAIRY-FREE

Prep time: 5 minutes • **Cook time:** 40 minutes

Yield: 4 servings

Peas are an excellent source of protein and fiber, and if you can digest them well, you'll want to include them in your healthy eating lifestyle. This creamy, thick stew is actually made without cream—the trick is in the micro-diced potatoes! I usually serve this dish with a simple shredded cabbage salad seasoned with salt, olive oil, and lemon, or with Roasted Red Pepper Salad (page 50). I also make this same stew without chicken, for a great plant-based side dish.

2 tablespoons extra-virgin olive oil

1 yellow onion, chopped

1 medium carrot, finely chopped

1 pound boneless, skinless chicken breast

1 pound frozen peas

1 small potato, peeled and finely chopped

1¼ teaspoons Himalayan salt

5 cups water

Spice it up!

½ to 1 teaspoon dill

1. In a medium stockpot, heat the olive oil over medium heat. Add the onions and carrots. Sauté until the onion is translucent.
2. Cut the chicken into small, bite-size cubes and add them to the pot. Sauté for about 5 minutes, until all sides are white and the chicken releases some water.
3. To the stockpot, add the peas, potatoes, salt, water, and dill (if using). Stir to combine, cover, and cook on low for 25 to 30 minutes.
4. Uncover, and cook for about 10 minutes uncovered. Most of the water will evaporate. Add the chicken to the stew, stir, and heat for 2 minutes.
5. Serve with freshly ground black pepper, if desired.

Continued ❯

Continued

* **Serving tip:** Try this stew with 1 tablespoon organic Greek yogurt.

* **Storage tip:** This stew can be stored in the refrigerator for 3 to 5 days.

* **Prep tip:** If you choose to make this without chicken, reduce the water to about 4 cups.

* **Seasonal tip:** When peas are in season, you can use fresh peas. Cooking time will remain the same. If you use "young peas," they will cook a bit faster.

Per serving: Calories: 338; Fat: 10g; Protein: 33g; Carbohydrates: 28g; Fiber: 8g; Sodium: 362mg

STRING BEAN CASSEROLE WITH CHICKEN

GLUTEN-FREE • SOY-FREE • NUT-FREE

Prep time: 5 minutes • **Cook time:** 45 minutes
Yield: 4 servings

When my mother-in-law came to visit, she asked to make baked string beans. I never liked string beans as a child, so I never made them as an adult, either. When she described the ingredients, the dish sounded delicious and nutritious—and it was! This lovely version is inspired by her recipe. It's rich in antioxidants, and the protein and fiber will keep you satiated for hours.

¼ cup extra-virgin olive oil

2 medium carrots, chopped

3 (4-ounce) boneless, skinless chicken breasts

1 pound fresh string beans, cut in half

3 cups water

1½ teaspoons Himalayan salt

2 large eggs

1 (6-ounce) container Greek yogurt

Spice it up!

½ teaspoon dried onion flakes

1. Preheat the oven to 425°F.
2. In a medium stockpot over medium heat, heat the olive oil. Add the carrots and dried onion flakes (if using). Sauté for about 1 minute, then add the chicken, stir, and cover. Let simmer for 5 minutes.
3. Add string beans, water, and salt. Stir, cover, and let simmer for about 25 minutes. The liquid should be reduced by half, and the beans should be fork-tender but not falling apart. Set aside.
4. Beat the eggs and mix with the yogurt until smooth.
5. Transfer everything from the pot to a baking dish.
6. Pour the egg mixture over the dish, stir, and bake for 20 to 25 minutes, or until the top is brown.

∗ **Serving tip:** A squeeze of lemon adds a nice flavor to this dish.

∗ **Substitution tip:** You can use frozen string beans instead of fresh. Cooking time will be about the same. You can also use fresh onions instead of dried onion flakes, if you prefer.

Per serving: Calories: 331; Fat: 20g; Protein: 26g; Carbohydrates: 13g; Fiber: 4g; Sodium: 457mg

BAKED BEANS IN TOMATO SAUCE

GLUTEN-FREE • NUT-FREE • SOY-FREE • VEGAN
Prep time: 10 minutes • **Cook time:** 30 minutes
Yield: 2 to 4 servings

Baked beans are quite different in taste in Europe than in the United States. Although they are more savory in Europe and cooked mainly in tomato sauce, in the United States, baked beans are on the sweeter side (molasses is used in a lot of recipes) and without the tomato base. They are both delicious in their own way, but I mainly make the tomato-based variety such as this recipe. Using canned beans cuts down on cooking time significantly. See page 9 to read about canned foods and what to look for when purchasing for your clean eating dishes.

2 tablespoons extra-virgin olive oil
1 yellow onion, chopped
1 teaspoon Himalayan salt
¼ teaspoon freshly ground black pepper
2 (13-ounce) cans cannellini beans, drained and rinsed
1 (13-ounce) can crushed tomatoes

Spice it up!
½ teaspoon basil
½ teaspoon oregano
Crushed red pepper flakes

1. Preheat the oven to 425°F.
2. In an oven-safe pot over medium heat, heat the olive oil. Add the onions. Sauté until the onions are translucent, then add the garlic, basil and oregano (if using), and salt and pepper. Cook for 1 minute.
3. Add the beans, followed by the tomatoes.
4. Transfer the pot to the oven and bake, covered, for 30 minutes. If desired, uncover the beans and turn the heat to broil for the last 3 minutes; just watch the beans closely so they don't burn.
5. Add some crushed red pepper on top of the beans if you like them spicy.

* **Serving tip:** Serve over rice alongside a green garden salad.

* **Substitution tip:** You can swap the cannellini beans for navy or white Italian beans.

Per serving: Calories: 567; Fat: 16g; Protein: 29g; Carbohydrates: 83g; Fiber: 28g; Sodium: 867mg

BEANS WITH BABY SPINACH

GLUTEN-FREE • NUT-FREE • SOY-FREE
Prep time: 5 minutes • **Cook time:** 15 minutes
Yield: 2 servings

This is what I call a "pantry edition" meal, because it mostly just calls for pantry items, such as canned beans, crushed tomatoes, and chicken or vegetable stock. It takes less than 5 minutes to put this together and then only 15 minutes to cook. Perfect for the busiest nights! I like white cannellini or butter beans for this dish, because they go well with both tomatoes and spinach. Enjoy this filling dish over some jasmine, basmati, or brown rice.

1 tablespoon extra-virgin olive oil
1 large garlic clove, minced
¾ cup crushed tomatoes
½ teaspoon dried basil
½ teaspoon Himalayan salt
1 (13-ounce) can white cannellini beans
½ cup chicken stock
2 cups baby spinach
Freshly ground black pepper (optional)

1. In a small saucepan over medium heat, heat the olive oil.
2. Add the garlic, then the tomatoes, basil, and salt, and cook for about 3 minutes.
3. Add the beans, stock, and spinach.
4. Cook for 10 more minutes. The liquid will reduce by half.
5. Sprinkle with some freshly ground black pepper, if desired.

✳ **Prep tip:** These beans warm up well, so they can be made a day in advance. When reheating, add ¼ cup chicken or vegetable stock and warm on the stovetop.

Per serving: Calories: 300; Fat: 8g; Protein: 17g; Carbohydrates: 44g; Fiber: 12g; Sodium: 333mg

ADZUKI BEAN SOUP

GLUTEN-FREE • NUT-FREE • SOY-FREE • VEGAN

Prep time: 5 minutes • **Cook time:** 30 minutes
Yield: 4 to 6 servings

Adzuki beans, also known as red mung beans, originated in China but are now grown throughout East Asia and the Himalayas. They have a great chewy, nutty texture as opposed to the softer red kidney or butter beans. They are a good source of iron, magnesium, potassium, folate, protein, and fiber. Studies show that adzuki beans are easier to digest than any other type of beans.

⅛ cup extra-virgin olive oil
1 leek, chopped
1 small yellow onion, finely chopped
1 large carrot, finely diced
1 long celery stalk, finely diced
1½ teaspoons Himalayan salt
2 (13-ounce) cans adzuki beans, drained and rinsed (see Substitution tip)
6 cups water

Spice it up!
2 bay leaves

1. In a medium saucepan over medium heat, heat the olive oil. Add the leeks, onions, carrots, and celery. Sauté for about 5 minutes.
2. Add the salt and bay leaves (if using), then add the beans and water.
3. Cover and cook over medium-low heat for about 30 minutes, until some of the water evaporates and the vegetables are cooked through. Shorten the cook time a little if you like thinner stew.
4. Remove the bay leaves and serve immediately.

* **Serving tip:** Cumin is another great add-in to this stew. Add ¼ teaspoon and work your way up. Add some minced fresh garlic for even richer taste.

* **Storage tip:** This dish can be stored in the refrigerator for about 3 days. Reheat it on the stovetop as desired. This soup may thicken a bit, so just add a little water before you warm it up.

* **Substitution tip:** You can use red kidney beans instead of adzuki.

Per serving: Calories: 301; Fat: 7g; Protein: 13g; Carbohydrates: 47g; Fiber: 13g; Sodium: 640mg

GREEN LENTIL STEW

Prep time: 5 minutes • **Cook time:** 30 minutes
Yield: 4 servings

Lentils are a wonderful source of plant protein and fiber, as well as magnesium, iron, and vitamin B$_6$. Green and red lentils are similar in taste and delicious, but they vary in their uses. Green lentils make good candidates for stews such as this one, for salads, or as salad toppers. Red lentils are great when making thicker, bisque-like soups; they soften fast, so they lose the chewy texture of the green lentils.

2 tablespoons extra-virgin olive oil
1 carrot, chopped
2 celery stalks, chopped
1 yellow onion, chopped
2 cups green lentils, rinsed
1 teaspoon Himalayan salt
6 cups water

Spice it up!
1 tablespoon cumin
Freshly ground black pepper

1. In a sauté pan or skillet over medium heat, heat the oil. Add the carrots, celery, and onion. Sauté until the onion is translucent.
2. Add the lentils, salt, cumin (if using), and water. Stir, cover, reduce heat to low, and cook for 25 to 30 minutes.
3. Add more salt and black pepper, if desired. Serve immediately, with a sprinkle of cumin, if desired.

* **Prep tip:** The lentils should become soft when cooked. In fact, don't worry if you overcook them—the soup is still delicious; it just won't have the chewiness. Sometimes I even prefer it that way.

Per serving: Calories: 418; Fat: 8g; Protein: 24g; Carbohydrates: 65g; Fiber: 12g; Sodium: 324mg

LENTIL BISQUE

GLUTEN-FREE • NUT-FREE • SOY-FREE • VEGETARIAN

Prep time: 5 minutes • **Cook time:** 25 minutes
Yield: 2 to 4 servings

This may be the easiest dish you will ever make. From start to finish, it takes 25 minutes, and your involvement is about 5 minutes. The best thing is, once you are done and you sit down to enjoy the bisque, you will love the outcome. So few ingredients, but savory and so nutritionally dense! Lentil bisque is a perfect lunch or snack. I suggest you enjoy it with a mixed greens salad or arugula with olive oil and lemon.

1 cup red lentils, washed and drained
1 yellow onion, chopped
2 garlic cloves, minced
¾ teaspoon Himalayan salt
4 cups water
¼ teaspoon freshly ground black pepper

Spice it up!
1½ teaspoons cumin

1. In a medium stockpot, combine the lentils, onion, garlic, salt, cumin (if using), and water.
2. Bring to a boil, cover, reduce heat to low and simmer for about 20 minutes.
3. You can serve it right away with freshly ground black pepper, or blend it for a smoother texture.

* **Substitution tip:** You can use finely chopped celery instead of onion.

Per serving: Calories: 370; Fat: 2g; Protein: 24g; Carbohydrates: 67g; Fiber: 11g; Sodium: 358mg

GREEN LENTIL SALAD WITH DIJON MUSTARD DRESSING

GLUTEN-FREE • NUT-FREE • SOY-FREE • VEGAN
Prep time: 5 minutes • **Cook time:** 15 minutes
Yield: 4 servings

The original idea for this recipe came from one of Gwyneth Paltrow's cookbooks, which I cook from often. This was the first time that I saw lentils prepared this way—cold and as a salad. The flavors seemed intriguing, so I tried the recipe. Little did I know, it would become one of my favorites, and I have been experimenting with different versions of it for years. This salad is clean and light, but perfect for any time of the year. Enjoy it as a main dish or as a side dish to any lean protein. I typically pair it with some tofu or some simple grilled turkey breast.

1 cup green lentils
2 cups arugula
½ red onion, thinly sliced
½ cup cherry tomatoes, halved
Freshly ground black pepper
1 batch Dijon Mustard Dressing (page 157)

1. To prepare lentils, boil them until tender, about 15 minutes. Drain and let them cool to room temperature.
2. In a bowl, combine the cooled lentils, arugula, onion, and tomatoes.
3. Add the dressing and lightly toss.
4. Add some freshly ground pepper and dressing on top, plus additional salt, if needed.

* **Ingredient tip:** You can buy jarred, cooked lentils; in that case, just drain and rinse them.

Per serving: Calories: 455; Fat: 22g; Protein: 19g; Carbohydrates: 50g; Fiber: 9g; Sodium: 251mg

SPICY SHRIMP PASTA ARRABBIATA

DAIRY-FREE • GLUTEN-FREE • NUT-FREE • SOY-FREE

Prep time: 5 minutes, plus 1 hour to marinate • **Cook time:** 15 minutes
Yield: 2 servings

I learned a little trick when it comes to shrimp, and every time I use it, the shrimp comes out perfect. If you marinate the shrimp in lemon or lime, it will actually cure; that is, cook without heat, so once you add it to your pasta sauce or grill, it only takes a few minutes to perfectly cook. Hearty whole-grain pasta pairs wonderfully with spicy tomato sauce and shrimp, but you can also try using lentil or chickpea pasta. All of these pastas are a little more nutrient-dense than traditional pasta, and because of their nuttier texture, the flavors are much deeper.

8 ounces raw shrimp, cleaned
2 tablespoons extra-virgin olive oil, divided
1 (13-ounce) can crushed tomatoes
2 garlic cloves minced, divided
Juice of ½ lemon
½ teaspoon Himalayan salt, divided
4 ounces whole-grain spaghetti

Spice it up!
¼ teaspoon crushed red pepper
½ teaspoon dried basil

1. In a resealable bag, combine the shrimp, 1 tablespoon of olive oil, crushed red pepper (if using), 1 minced garlic clove, lemon juice, and salt. Mix and let marinate on the kitchen counter for about 1 hour.
2. In a large, nonstick sauté pan or skillet over medium heat, heat the remaining tablespoon of oil. Add the shrimp, reserving the liquid in the bag. Cook for 1 minute on each side, just until the shrimp becomes pinkish.
3. Add the remaining minced garlic clove, tomatoes, reserved liquid from the shrimp, ¼ teaspoon of salt and basil (if using). Cook for about 4 minutes, gently shaking the pan occasionally.
4. Meanwhile, cook the pasta according to instructions for al dente. Drain the spaghetti, reserving ¼ cup of the liquid.
5. Add the pasta and reserved liquid to the pan with the shrimp and toss. Cook for about 2 minutes so some of the liquid evaporates and the flavors marinate.

* **Serving tip:** If you like dishes extra spicy, add some more crushed red pepper on top. Fresh basil adds a nice touch, too.

* **Substitution tip:** You can use whole peeled tomatoes—just crush them with your hands and add all the liquid from the can.

Per serving: Calories: 451; Fat: 15g; Protein: 26g; Carbohydrates: 55g; Fiber: 6g; Sodium: 765mg

CREAMY CHICKEN AND BROCCOLI PASTA

NUT-FREE • SOY-FREE
Prep time: 5 minutes • **Cook time:** 20 minutes
Yield: 4 servings

This pasta dish is simple and a family favorite. It's inspired by my friend Ana, who showed me how to make a version of this dish over 10 years ago. Although I've modified it many times, it has never left my kitchen. It is that good! This pasta combines all that we need in a healthy meal—protein, fiber, and good fats, plus it's a wonderful dish if you need to "hide" any veggies from your kids' eyes. C'mon, most of us have had to do this at one time or another. Instead of adding broccoli, you can finely grate zucchini—I promise it will go unnoticed.

8 ounces whole-grain pasta, such as rigatoni
2 tablespoons extra-virgin olive oil
1 pound chicken breast, diced
2 cup broccoli, cut into small florets
½ teaspoon Himalayan salt
½ cup water, divided
2 tablespoons pesto
2 tablespoons plain vegan cream cheese (see Substitution tip)

Spice it up!
¼ teaspoon garlic powder
¼ teaspoon dried onion flakes

1. Cook the pasta according to package instructions. Reserve ¼ cup of the cooking liquid.
2. Meanwhile, in a medium sauté pan or skillet over medium heat, heat the oil.
3. Add the chicken, and garlic powder and dried onion flakes (if using), and stir. Add the broccoli, salt, and ¼ cup of water. Cover and cook for a few minutes, until the chicken turns white.
4. When about half the water has evaporated, add the pesto and remaining ¼ cup of water. Cover and cook for another 3 to 4 minutes.
5. Stir in the cream cheese and leave the pan uncovered.
6. Turn off the heat.
7. Add the cooked pasta and ¼ cup of reserved liquid. Stir together to coat.
8. Serve immediately.

＊ **Substitution tip:** Mascarpone cheese works well in this recipe in place of the vegan cream cheese. You can use scallions or yellow onion instead of dried onion flakes. Fresh garlic may be used instead of garlic powder.

Per serving: Calories: 467; Fat: 16g; Protein: 37g; Carbohydrates: 46g; Fiber: 6g; Sodium: 347mg

Buddha Bowl
page 110

CHAPTER SIX

PLANT-BASED MEALS

Several years ago, I realized that most of our meals were based on animal protein and everything else revolved around that. The plate would contain meat and some kind of starch, and then we would "throw in" some veggies. What I realized while studying nutrition is that those types of meals are not well balanced. Fiber and antioxidants play a huge role in our health, and those elements are not found in meats, but rather in plants. Once I shifted gears and vegetables became my focus, the plates started looking much more balanced. Think about a rainbow: The more colors you see on your plate, the better! Lead with veggies, then add some protein (animal- or plant-based), then some grains. In this chapter, I am sharing some of my favorite plant-based meals that are really easy to make. Some can be eaten as a main, and others you can use as side dishes for your meat or seafood dishes. All the clean recipes in this chapter are nutrient-dense, filling, and very satisfying.

Collard Green Wraps with Vegetables and Tahini Dressing   101

Kale and Bean Soup with Tofu   102

Crispy Baked Tofu   103

Teriyaki Tofu   104

Roasted Cauliflower with Quinoa and Mustard Dressing   105

Veggie Cauliflower Rice   106

Mashed Sweet Potatoes with Spinach   107

Quinoa Tabbouleh   108

Quinoa Burrito Bowl   109

* Buddha Bowl   110

Vegan Tacos   111

Eggplant Parm   112

Cauliflower Chickpea Stew with Turmeric   113

Tandoori Cauliflower Curry   114

Rosemary Zucchini Tomato Bake   115

Cold Pasta Salad   116

Chickpea Pasta with Mushrooms and Sage   117

Vegan Lasagna   119

Spaghetti Squash with Vegan Bolognese   120

COLLARD GREEN WRAPS WITH VEGETABLES AND TAHINI DRESSING

DAIRY-FREE · GLUTEN-FREE · NUT-FREE · SOY-FREE · VEGAN
Prep time: 10 minutes · **Cook time:** 15 minutes
Yield: 2 servings

These wraps make a lovely light lunch or snack to share with someone. You can use any veggies you choose inside the wraps. I suggest raw veggies, such as shredded carrots, shredded purple cabbage, and avocado. No matter what, use the tahini dressing to dip! You can also spread hummus, then add sweet potato, avocado, and cucumber, wrap it up, and enjoy.

1 small sweet potato, roasted, cut into 6 wedges
1 teaspoon extra-virgin olive oil
6 collard green leaves, blanched (see method in step 4, page 81)
½ English cucumber, sliced lengthwise into 6 sticks
½ avocado, sliced into 6 slices
⅓ cup Tahini Dressing (page 156)

1. Preheat the oven to 425°F.
2. On a baking sheet, toss the potato wedges with the oil. Bake for about 15 minutes.
3. In the wide bottom part of a blanched collard leaf, add one cucumber, one sweet potato wedge, and one avocado slice. Start rolling at the wide end toward the top, and when you get one-third of the way up, fold the two sides toward the center to close off the edges, and then continue wrapping until done. Place seam-side down on a serving plate. Repeat with the remaining greens and fillings.
4. Serve with tahini dressing.

✳ **Substitution tip:** You can use Swiss chard or beet greens instead of collard greens.

Per serving: Calories: 325; Fat: 22g; Protein: 7g; Carbohydrates: 32g; Fiber: 12g; Sodium: 144mg

KALE AND BEAN SOUP WITH TOFU

DAIRY-FREE · GLUTEN-FREE · NUT-FREE · VEGAN
Prep time: 5 minutes · **Cook time:** 25 minutes
Yield: 4 servings

This soup comes together so easily if you have all the items in your pantry. It will keep you full for hours to come. Tofu, beans, and kale are all rich in protein, and kale and beans are also packed with fiber. As a quick reminder, always pick tofu that carries a non-GMO label. Also, tofu doesn't last long once opened, and kale can get soggy in soups, so you'll want to enjoy this soup either freshly made or within a day.

3 tablespoons extra-virgin olive oil
1 large yellow onion, thinly sliced
4 cups kale, coarsely chopped
1 (13-ounce) can cannellini beans, rinsed and drained
4 cups vegetable stock
4 cups water
1 (14-ounce) package extra-firm tofu, drained and cubed
1 teaspoon Himalayan salt

Spice it up!
½ teaspoon garlic powder
½ teaspoon crushed red pepper flakes

1. In a medium saucepan over medium heat, heat the olive oil. Add the onion and sauté until translucent.
2. Add the kale, beans, stock, and water, and bring it to a boil. Add the tofu, salt, and garlic powder (if using). Cook for about 20 minutes, partly covered.
3. Add some red pepper chili flakes before serving (if using).

* **Storage tip:** Store leftovers in a glass container in the refrigerator. Although it doesn't last long, this soup is even better the next day, once the flavors marinate overnight.

* **Substitution tip:** You can use Swiss chard or collard greens instead of kale. Red kidney beans can be used instead of cannellini.

Per serving: Calories: 302; Fat: 17g; Protein: 18g; Carbohydrates: 25g; Fiber: 7g; Sodium: 433mg

CRISPY BAKED TOFU

DAIRY-FREE • GLUTEN-FREE • NUT-FREE • SOY-FREE • VEGAN
Prep time: 5 minutes • **Cook time:** 30 minutes
Yield: 2 servings

There are so many different ways to prepare tofu, from lightly panfrying it to adding it to soups to baking it in the oven. Because tofu is neutral in taste, it will pick up any flavors you marinate it in. The marinades can be spice rubs, such as the one in this recipe, or a combination of soy sauce, rice vinegar, sesame oil, and garlic. For a super quick version, I marinate tofu in a teriyaki glaze before panfrying or baking it. The longer you marinate the tofu, the more flavor it will have.

1 (14-ounce) package extra-firm tofu
¼ teaspoon garlic powder
¼ teaspoon ginger powder
¼ teaspoon Himalayan salt
2 tablespoons sesame oil

1. Preheat the oven to 425°F. Line a baking sheet with parchment paper and set aside.
2. Drain the tofu. Cut it lengthwise into rectangles, about 1 finger length. Wrap it in three sheets of paper towels and put in a colander for 10 minutes.
3. To prepare the spice rub, mix the garlic powder, ginger, and salt.
4. Put the tofu in a shallow bowl. Sprinkle each slice of tofu with some spice rub. Drizzle with the sesame oil and rub well until well coated.
5. Lay out the tofu slices on the prepared baking sheet. Sprinkle sesame seeds on top (if using). If using chili flakes, add them as well.
6. Bake until the tofu becomes crispy, about 30 minutes.

* **Prep tip:** You can prepare the spice rub the night before. You can also cut the tofu, wrap it in paper towels, and store it in the refrigerator overnight. I do not recommend baking the tofu and saving it for the next day, as tofu is best enjoyed as soon as it's prepared.

* **Ingredient tip:** Always choose extra-firm tofu if you are preparing it in the oven or in a pan, because it holds up better. For soups, you can use any type of tofu.

* **Substitution tip:** If you have a sesame allergy, you may omit sesame seeds altogether and use olive oil instead of sesame oil.

Per serving: Calories: 303; Fat: 25g; Protein: 20g; Carbohydrates: 4g; Fiber: 1g; Sodium: 171mg

TERIYAKI TOFU

DAIRY-FREE • NUT-FREE • VEGAN
Prep time: 15 minutes • **Cook time:** 15 minutes
Yield: 2 servings

The glaze in this recipe also works well with chicken or salmon. The glaze, when added to tofu or meats, becomes more subtle and is not overwhelming. That said, the longer you marinate the ingredients, the more flavor it will pick up. This is especially true with tofu which I suggest marinating for at least 30 minutes.

2 tablespoons soy sauce
1 tablespoon raw honey
1 garlic clove, minced
¼ teaspoon ground ginger
1 (10-ounce) package extra-firm tofu, drained and cubed
1 tablespoon extra-virgin olive oil
¼ teaspoon Himalayan salt

Spice it up!
1 tablespoon sesame seeds

1. In a small bowl, whisk together the soy sauce, honey, garlic, and ginger. Add the tofu, mix well, and let it marinate for about 15 minutes, stirring halfway through.
2. Take the tofu out of the marinade and reserve the liquid.
3. In a nonstick sauté pan or skillet over medium heat, heat the oil. Add the tofu. Cook for about 6 minutes, flipping the tofu after about 3 minutes.
4. Add the reserved marinade to the pan and continue cooking. Toss with sesame seeds (if using).
5. Cook until the marinade evaporates.
6. Serve warm.

* **Serving tip:** Serve tofu with jasmine rice and stir-fried veggies or over your favorite salad. Teriyaki tofu goes really well with some of the dishes from chapters 5 and 6, such as Veggie Cauliflower Rice (page 106), Buddha Bowl (page 110), or Vegetable Fried Rice (page 80).

* **Substitution tips:** You can use ½ teaspoon minced fresh ginger instead of the ground ginger. Coconut aminos can be used instead of soy sauce.

Per serving: Calories: 232; Fat: 15g; Protein: 15g; Carbohydrates: 13g; Fiber: 1g; Sodium: 1091mg

ROASTED CAULIFLOWER WITH QUINOA AND MUSTARD DRESSING

DAIRY-FREE · GLUTEN-FREE · NUT-FREE · SOY-FREE · VEGAN

Prep time: 5 minutes · **Cook time:** 30 minutes
Yield: 4 servings

This dish can be eaten by itself or served as a side dish to any lean protein. This family-friendly recipe is a wonderful addition when you are hosting barbecues or big dinner parties. It's simple to make, yet looks and sounds so complex. The secret is in the mustard dressing, which adds flavor and depth to the cauliflower.

1 serving Tangy Mustard Dressing with Apple Cider Vinegar (page 158)
1 small head cauliflower, broken into small florets
1 tablespoon extra-virgin olive oil
½ teaspoon Himalayan salt
½ cup cooked quinoa

1. Whisk the dressing and set aside.
2. Preheat the oven to 425°F. Line a baking sheet with parchment paper.
3. Spread the cauliflower florets on the baking sheet and gently toss with the oil and salt to coat.
4. Bake until golden, about 30 minutes.
5. Put the cauliflower in a bowl. Add the quinoa and stir to combine.
6. Add the dressing and toss lightly.

✴ **Serving tip:** Sprinkle with fresh parsley and black pepper, if desired.

✴ **Substitution tip:** You can use white wine vinegar instead of apple cider vinegar.

Per serving: Calories: 84; Fat: 5g; Protein: 2g; Carbohydrates: 8g; Fiber: 2g; Sodium: 203mg

VEGGIE CAULIFLOWER RICE

DAIRY-FREE · GLUTEN-FREE · NUT-FREE · VEGAN
Prep time: 5 minutes · **Cook time:** 30 minutes
Yield: 2 servings

There's a growing interest in recipes that are dairy-free, grain-free, and gluten-free. Grains trigger inflammation in some individuals, so it's nice that there are delicious alternatives. Making rice out of cauliflower is a recent trend, and I am a huge fan! To make this rice out of cauliflower, all you need to do is grate it on a grater. Use the side with the biggest holes, as the smallest holes may make it mushy. You can really get creative as far as vegetables you add to this dish—just start with onion and garlic, then add anything else you like.

1 tablespoon extra-virgin olive oil
1 scallion, green and white parts, chopped
2½ cups cauliflower rice
1 cup shiitake mushrooms, chopped
1 cup carrots, shredded
½ teaspoon Himalayan salt
1 cup water
1 tablespoon soy sauce
Freshly ground black pepper (optional)

1. In a medium sauté pan or skillet over medium heat, heat the oil. When it is warm, add the scallions.
2. After about 1 minute, add the cauliflower, mushrooms, carrots, salt, and water.
3. Cover, reduce heat to low, and cook for 15 minutes.
4. Add the soy sauce, cover, and continue cooking until all the liquid evaporates, about 15 minutes.
5. Add some fresh black pepper, if desired.

* **Substitution tip:** You can use any kinds of mushrooms. The scallion can be replaced with 1 shallot, thinly sliced. Soy sauce can be replaced with coconut aminos.

* **Serving tip:** Stirring in an egg at the very end of cooking makes this dish taste like real fried rice.

Per serving: Calories: 133; Fat: 7g; Protein: 5g; Carbohydrates: 14g; Fiber: 5g; Sodium: 869mg

MASHED SWEET POTATOES WITH SPINACH

DAIRY-FREE · GLUTEN-FREE · NUT-FREE · SOY-FREE · VEGAN
Prep time: 5 minutes · **Cook time:** 15 minutes
Yield: 2 servings

Sweet potatoes are not nutritionally superior to white potatoes, as many may believe. Each has its benefits, and unless you need to watch your glycemic index, both have a place in a clean eating lifestyle. Similar in calories, carbohydrate, and fat content, both varieties contain some protein and fiber. While sweet potatoes are higher in fiber, white potatoes are higher in protein. Both kinds of potatoes contain vitamin C and potassium. One advantage of sweet potatoes is that they are a great source of vitamin A for immunity and vision. Enjoy your taters with spinach in this colorful dish.

2 medium sweet potatoes, cubed
2 tablespoons extra-virgin olive oil
3 cups baby spinach
4 tablespoons unsweetened, plant-based milk, such as almond milk
½ teaspoon Himalayan salt

Spice it up!
½ teaspoon garlic powder

1. In a medium saucepan, put in the sweet potatoes and just enough water to cover the potatoes. Bring to a boil and cook until sweet potatoes are fork-tender, about 15 minutes.
2. Drain the potatoes and mash with a fork. Set aside.
3. Meanwhile, in a small nonstick pan, heat the oil and add the spinach. Sauté for just 1 minute, then add the mashed potatoes, milk, salt, and garlic powder (if using).
4. Cook for 3 minutes to combine the flavors.
5. Remove from heat and serve warm.

* **Prep tip:** As potatoes generally do not reheat well, feel free to modify the recipe to make smaller portions that you know you will eat the same day.

Per serving: Calories: 255; Fat: 14g; Protein: 4g; Carbohydrates: 29g; Fiber: 5g; Sodium: 440mg

QUINOA TABBOULEH

DAIRY-FREE · GLUTEN-FREE · NUT-FREE · SOY-FREE · VEGAN
Prep time: 10 minutes
Yield: 4 to 6 servings

I often find myself with leftover rice or quinoa, and typically after day one, nobody feels like having it anymore; it just tastes dry and bland. So I find ways to use the leftovers and create a brand-new dish. This quinoa tabbouleh is one of those "makeover" dishes. Adding fresh herbs to grains always takes them to a new level. This dish is also great for larger dinner parties; everyone loves seeing fresh greens on the table. The best part about this tabbouleh is that you can make it a day in advance and just add the dressing when ready to serve.

2 cups cooked quinoa
1¼ cups fresh parsley, chopped
1 large red onion, chopped
3 Persian cucumbers, cut into small cubes
¼ cup extra-virgin olive oil
Juice of ½ large lemon
½ teaspoon Himalayan salt

Spice it up!
1 tablespoon dried mint flakes

1. In a large bowl, combine the quinoa, parsley, dried mint (if using), onion, and cucumbers.
2. In a small bowl, whisk together oil, lemon juice, and salt and add it to the large bowl. Toss until everything is evenly coated.

* **Substitution tip:** You can use ½ English cucumber instead of Persian cucumbers. You may also use scallions or shallots instead of red onion. Try ¼ cup of fresh mint instead of dry. If you use fresh mint, add only 1 cup fresh parsley.

* **Prep tip:** If you do not have cooked quinoa, just use the basic steps to cook it: Bring 4 cups of water to a boil, add 2 cups of quinoa, cover, and cook on low for about 20 minutes. The quinoa-to-water ratio is always 1:2.

Per serving: Calories: 276; Fat: 16g; Protein: 6g; Carbohydrates: 30g; Fiber: 5g; Sodium: 167mg

QUINOA BURRITO BOWL

DAIRY-FREE · GLUTEN-FREE · NUT-FREE · SOY-FREE · VEGAN

Prep time: 5 minutes · **Cook time:** 15 minutes

Yield: 2 servings

Restaurant burritos can be quite heavy on your digestion due to big tortilla wraps and heavy sauces. Making one at home is really so much healthier. As far as ingredients go, you do not need to limit yourself to those listed here. Swap out the avocado for fresh green pepper, or the beans for chickpeas. Because you are serving this in a bowl, there is no need for a tortilla. But if you would like to have one, I suggest getting a whole-grain tortilla and also adding some iceberg lettuce inside.

1 cup water

½ cup red quinoa, uncooked, rinsed

1 cup canned red kidney beans, drained and rinsed

½ small red onion, thinly sliced

½ avocado, cubed

½ teaspoon Himalayan salt

1 tablespoon extra-virgin olive oil

Juice of ½ lemon, squeezed

1. In a small saucepan, bring the water to a boil. Add the quinoa, cover, and cook on low heat for about 15 minutes. Transfer the quinoa to a salad bowl and let it cool down to room temperature.
2. Add the beans, onion, and avocado to the cooled quinoa. Add the salt, olive oil, and lemon juice and toss lightly.

* **Serving tip:** Top with some fresh parsley or cilantro, if desired.

* **Substitution tip:** You can use shallots instead of red onion, black beans instead of kidney beans, and/or white quinoa instead of red.

Per serving: Calories: 426; Fat: 17g; Protein: 16g; Carbohydrates: 55g; Fiber: 16g; Sodium: 300mg

BUDDHA BOWL

DAIRY-FREE · GLUTEN-FREE · NUT-FREE · SOY-FREE · VEGAN
Prep time: 5 minutes
Yield: 1 to 2 servings

Buddha bowls are a wonderful way to use up any leftovers you have in your refrigerator or pantry—get creative! Building a "proper" Buddha bowl is quite easy if you shoot for adding as many colors as you can. In this recipe, we almost have a full rainbow. Kale is a wonderful base for Buddha bowls because it is hearty and substantial. It's also higher in fiber than most other greens. Kale just needs to be massaged well with your hands in order to make it softer and easier to digest.

4 cups kale, washed
¼ cup black-eyed beans, rinsed and drained
½ cup English cucumber, cubed
½ avocado, chopped
1 small red onion, thinly sliced

Spice it up!
Basic EVOO and Lemon Dressing (page 154)

1. In a large shallow bowl, put in the kale and half of the dressing (if using).
2. Massage the kale with your hands until soft.
3. Add the black beans, cucumber, avocado, onion, and the rest of the dressing. Lightly toss.
4. If you wish, add some sunflower or hemp seeds on top.

* **Serving tip:** This bowl also works well with Dijon Mustard Dressing (page 157) or Tahini Dressing (page 156).

* **Substitution tip:** This recipe is just a template—use your imagination and whatever you have in your refrigerator. You can replace the black-eyed beans with black beans, and you can add carrots, snap peas, mushrooms, olives, roasted nuts, cooked grains—the sky's the limit.

Per serving: Calories: 481; Fat: 31g; Protein: 16g; Carbohydrates: 45g; Fiber: 20g; Sodium: 363mg

VEGAN TACOS

DAIRY-FREE · GLUTEN-FREE · NUT-FREE · SOY-FREE · VEGAN
Prep time: 10 minutes · **Cook time:** 5 minutes
Yield: 2 to 3 servings

Traditionally, tacos are made with ground beef, but I like making them with ground turkey or tofu. It is all about the toppings and that good-old taco spice. Unfortunately, store-bought taco spice is usually loaded with artificial ingredients and colors. I created a simple recipe for taco spice, so you do not need to buy one at the grocery store anymore. This version of tacos is light and perfect for warmer days.

1 (14-ounce) package extra-firm tofu, drained
1 tablespoon Taco Seasoning (page 9)
3 tablespoons extra-virgin olive oil, divided, plus more if needed
5 cups shredded coleslaw and carrot mix
Juice of ½ large lemon
½ teaspoon Himalayan salt
4 to 6 organic corn tortillas

1. Drain the tofu and wrap it in a triple layer of paper towels for a few minutes so it can dry out. Cut the tofu into thick slices.
2. In a large resealable bag, combine the tofu slices, taco seasoning, and 1 tablespoon of olive oil. Mix well and let marinate at room temperature for at least 20 minutes.
3. Meanwhile, in a large bowl, combine the coleslaw mix, lemon juice, salt, and 1 tablespoon of oil. Mix well with your hands. The more you massage the cabbage, the softer it will become. Set it aside.
4. In a small, nonstick sauté pan or skillet over medium heat, heat the remaining tablespoon of oil. Working in batches, if needed, add the tofu slices and panfry for 3 minutes. Flip and cook for 2 minutes on the other side. Add another teaspoon of oil as needed.
5. Take tofu out of the pan and let it cool for 1 to 2 minutes.
6. Using the same pan, warm the tortillas one by one. Alternatively, you can warm them on the open fire if you have a gas stove.
7. To each tortilla, add some tofu and coleslaw mix. Sprinkle with extra taco seasoning if desired.

* **Serving tip:** Top with some fresh cilantro for additional flavor.

* **Substitution tip:** You can use wheat tortillas or butter (Boston) lettuce for the wraps.

Per serving: Calories: 533; Fat: 33g; Protein: 25g; Carbohydrates: 42g; Fiber: 9g; Sodium: 437mg

EGGPLANT PARM

DAIRY-FREE • GLUTEN-FREE • NUT-FREE • SOY-FREE • VEGAN

Prep time: 5 minutes · **Cook time:** 30 minutes
Yield: 2 servings

Eggplant contains a lot of water, so you'll want to take some of the water out before baking it. Here's how: Cut the eggplant into slices, then lay them out on three sheets of paper towels. Sprinkle some salt on top and then add another layer of paper towels. Let it drain for about 30 minutes. Now get ready to enjoy some delicious eggplant Parm!

1 large eggplant, peeled and cut into thick slices
Olive oil spray
1 (13-ounce) jar marinara sauce
4 tablespoons shredded vegan mozzarella
2 tablespoons fresh basil, chopped
½ teaspoon Himalayan salt

1. Preheat the oven to 400°F.
2. Line a deep baking dish with parchment paper and set aside.
3. Prepare the eggplant as described above.
4. Once the eggplant is prepared, add the first layer to the baking dish. Use the largest slices for the bottom layer. Top each eggplant round with some marinara, shredded mozzarella, and fresh basil. Add the second layer of eggplant rounds, then repeat with the marinara, mozzarella, and basil. Finally, add the third layer of eggplant rounds, marinara, mozzarella, and basil.
5. If desired, add some black pepper and oregano, and spray the top with olive oil.
6. Bake until the cheese is bubbly and eggplant is soft, about 30 minutes.

* **Prep tip:** You can grill the eggplant for a few minutes on each side before layering it. I often make this dish when I have leftover grilled eggplant from the barbecue.

* **Substitution tip:** You can use dry basil instead of fresh. Just sprinkle some on each layer over the marinara sauce.

Per serving: Calories: 153; Fat: 3g; Protein: 10g; Carbohydrates: 26g; Fiber: 11g; Sodium: 286mg

CAULIFLOWER CHICKPEA STEW WITH TURMERIC

DAIRY-FREE • GLUTEN-FREE • NUT-FREE • SOY-FREE • VEGAN

Prep time: 5 minutes • **Cook time:** 45 minutes
Yield: 4 servings

This soup fits the bill for anti-inflammatory and cleansing properties for more than one reason. While turmeric is one of the strongest antioxidants there is, cauliflower is not far behind in its healing qualities. The two together in this soup make a wonderful pair. This stew is filling and soothing, and the turmeric is not overpowering. I suggest you enjoy this soup any time you feel like you need to reset your body and start fresh.

½ head cauliflower, cut into small florets
1 (13-ounce) can chickpeas, rinsed and drained
1 yellow onion, thinly sliced
1 medium leek, thinly sliced
1 teaspoon Himalayan salt
½ teaspoon turmeric
¼ teaspoon freshly ground black pepper
6 cups water

Spice it up!
½ teaspoon garlic powder

1. In a medium stockpot, combine the cauliflower, chickpeas, onion, leek, salt, turmeric, pepper, garlic powder (if using), and water.
2. Bring to a boil, cover, and cook for 30 minutes. Uncover and cook for another 15 minutes.
3. Serve immediately, as is, or over some cooked brown rice.

* **Storage tip:** Store leftover stew in a glass container in the refrigerator for up to 2 days.

Per serving: Calories: 138; Fat: 2g; Protein: 7g; Carbohydrates: 25g; Fiber: 6g; Sodium: 471mg

TANDOORI CAULIFLOWER CURRY

DAIRY-FREE · GLUTEN-FREE · NUT-FREE · SOY-FREE · VEGAN

Prep time: 5 minutes · **Cook time:** 25 minutes
Yield: 4 servings

Indian dishes are usually full of flavor. I especially like to use Indian spices when making vegetables because these spices add depth and elevate the veggies to another level of deliciousness. This very simple and quick version of curried cauliflower uses ready-made curry paste. Typical ingredients found in tandoori curry paste include coriander, basil, ginger, cardamom, garlic, turmeric, tomato paste, and coconut oil. Talk about an explosion of flavors!

½ head cauliflower, broken into small florets
1 tablespoon extra-virgin olive oil
1 yellow onion, sliced
2 garlic cloves, minced
1 zucchini, cubed
2 to 3 tablespoons tandoori curry paste
¼ teaspoon Himalayan salt

Spice it up!
¼ cup fresh coriander

1. In a pot of water, cook the cauliflower florets until tender, about 5 minutes. Reserve about 2 cups of the cooking liquid.
2. In a large saucepan over medium heat, heat the olive oil. Add the onion and garlic. Sauté for about 2 minutes.
3. Add the zucchini and sauté for another 3 minutes.
4. Add the cauliflower, reserved liquid, curry paste, and salt. Stir, cover, and cook for about 15 minutes.
5. Serve with fresh coriander, if desired.

✳ **Serving tip:** This dish is best served over some jasmine or brown rice, but you can also enjoy it with chickpeas.

✳ **Substitution tip:** Try fresh parsley instead of the coriander.

Per serving: Calories: 66; Fat: 4g; Protein: 2g; Carbohydrates: 7g; Fiber: 3g; Sodium: 94mg

ROSEMARY ZUCCHINI TOMATO BAKE

DAIRY-FREE • GLUTEN-FREE • NUT-FREE • SOY-FREE • VEGAN
Prep time: 5 minutes • **Cook time:** 30 minutes
Yield: 2 to 4 servings

This is one of the first dishes I remember my mom making when I moved to the United States. As a massage therapist, she led a very holistic lifestyle, which I don't think I understood at the time. She loved making and eating dishes like this, but for me this was "too healthy" and not substantial enough. Looking back, I wish I had embraced her way of living right then and there. This dish is wonderfully light and wholesome.

1 medium potato, thinly sliced
1 large red heirloom tomato, sliced into thick rounds
1 zucchini, cut into thick rounds
1 teaspoon Himalayan salt
1 teaspoon dried rosemary
1 tablespoon extra-virgin olive oil

1. Preheat the oven to 400°F.
2. Line a small baking sheet with parchment paper.
3. Layer the potatoes all around the edges. Then layer the tomatoes inside the potatoes, followed by the zucchini in the center. Sprinkle salt as you lay out each layer.
4. Sprinkle the rosemary on top and drizzle with olive oil.
5. Bake for 20 minutes, then turn the oven to either convection bake or broil for the last 5 minutes. If you are using the broiler, watch it closely as it can quickly burn.

✳ **Substitution tip:** I used rosemary as the main spice, but you can use any dried herb of your choice, including herbs de Provence or oregano. You can also use plum tomatoes instead of heirloom; just use about 4 small ones, cut into thick rounds.

Per serving: Calories: 175; Fat: 7g; Protein: 4g; Carbohydrates: 25g; Fiber: 5g; Sodium: 854mg

COLD PASTA SALAD

DAIRY-FREE • GLUTEN-FREE • NUT-FREE • SOY-FREE • VEGAN

Prep time: 10 minutes • **Cook time:** 10 minutes
Yield: 2 servings

This pasta is wonderful for big dinner parties and outdoor barbecues; a true crowd pleaser! I especially like to prepare it in summer months when plenty of fresh herbs and seasonal veggies are available.

1 cup whole-grain rotini pasta
¼ cup black olives
¼ cup finely chopped cucumbers
1 tablespoon minced yellow onion
¼ teaspoon Himalayan salt
2 tablespoons Tangy Mustard Dressing with Apple Cider Vinegar (page 158)

Spice it up!
1 tablespoon chopped, fresh basil

1. Cook the pasta according to package instructions for al dente. Let it cool to room temperature.
2. In a bowl, combine the pasta with the olives, cucumbers, onions, and salt.
3. Add the dressing and toss to combine.
4. Add fresh basil on top, if desired, and serve immediately.

* **Ingredient tip:** This recipe is a great use for leftover pasta. If the pasta has dried out and is tough, bring some water to a boil and add the pasta for a few seconds so it warms up and softens. Proceed with the recipe as directed.

* **Seasonal tip:** When tomatoes are in season, add ¼ cup finely chopped tomatoes to this dish.

* **Substitution tip:** You can swap out the onion for shallots.

Per serving: Calories: 225; Fat: 9g; Protein: 7g; Carbohydrates: 32g; Fiber: 5g; Sodium: 368mg

CHICKPEA PASTA WITH MUSHROOMS AND SAGE

DAIRY-FREE · GLUTEN-FREE · NUT-FREE · SOY-FREE · VEGAN
Prep time: 5 minutes · **Cook time:** 15 minutes
Yield: 4 servings

This pasta is so creamy you would think there is actual cream inside. The trick is in the riced cauliflower and non-dairy cream cheese. If you can't find riced cauliflower, you can simply grate the cauliflower with a grater. Also, I used almond milk cream cheese but you can replace it with any non-dairy cream cheese of your choice.

3 tablespoons extra-virgin olive oil
1 cup raw riced cauliflower
4 ounces shiitake mushrooms, sliced
1 tablespoon fresh sage, chopped
½ teaspoon Himalayan salt, plus more if needed
¼ cup water
2 tablespoons plain almond milk cream cheese
8 ounces chickpea pasta

Spice it up!
¼ teaspoon garlic powder
¼ teaspoon dried onion flakes
Truffle oil

1. In a medium sauté pan or skillet over medium heat, heat the olive oil.
2. Add the cauliflower and mushrooms, and garlic powder and dried onion flakes (if using). Sauté for about 2 minutes, then add the fresh sage, salt, and water. Cover, reduce heat to low, and cook for about 5 minutes.
3. Stir in the cream cheese, and cook uncovered for about 2 minutes, just until everything looks incorporated. Set aside.
4. Cook pasta according to instructions. Drain, reserving ¼ cup of the cooking liquid.
5. Add the pasta and reserved liquid to the mushroom mixture. Cook for just 1 minute until the flavors combine. Taste for saltiness and add more, if needed.
6. Serve drizzled with some truffle oil, if desired.

Continued ❯

Continued

＊ **Substitution tip:** I like shiitake mushrooms because of their chewy texture, but you can use any mushrooms you like. I used chickpea pasta in this recipe, but you can use whole-grain, spelt, or lentil pasta, or any other pasta of your liking. You can also use fresh onion and garlic in place of the onion flakes and garlic powder. Use ½ small yellow onion and 2 garlic cloves.

Per serving: Calories: 320; Fat: 16g; Protein: 15g; Carbohydrates: 36g; Fiber: 7g; Sodium: 234mg

VEGAN LASAGNA

DAIRY-FREE · GLUTEN-FREE · NUT-FREE · SOY-FREE · VEGAN

Prep time: 5 minutes · **Cook time:** 25 minutes
Yield: 4 servings

I love this plant-based lasagna so much that I just had to develop a simplified version of it for this clean eating cookbook. While I love traditional lasagna, this one packs so much flavor and is far more nutritious. I chose spinach for this recipe, but you can add any veggies you like. Zucchini and peppers are great, as well as mushrooms and onions. Try this version first, and then go ahead and get creative!

2 tablespoons extra-virgin olive oil
3 cups baby spinach
8 ounces tofu, drained and crumbled
1 tablespoon Mediterranean Blend (page 9)
½ teaspoon Himalayan salt
1 (13-ounce) can tomato sauce or puree
1 box lasagna sheets
Shredded vegan mozzarella (optional)
Freshly ground black pepper

1. Preheat the oven to 400°F.
2. Line an 8-by-8-inch baking dish with parchment paper. Set aside.
3. In a small, nonstick sauté pan or skillet over medium heat, heat the olive oil. Add the spinach and cook for about 1 minute. Add the crumbled tofu, spice blend, and salt, and stir to combine.
4. Add the tomato sauce, stir, and cook for another 2 to 3 minutes. Set aside.
5. Lay the lasagna sheets on the bottom of the prepared baking dish, then add a quarter of the sauce. Top with one-third of the spinach and tofu mixture. Repeat with several layers, ending with sauce on top. Add some shredded vegan mozzarella cheese on top, if desired, as well as some black pepper.
6. Bake for 30 minutes.
7. Let the lasagna cool before cutting it.

✳ **Substitution tip:** You can use Swiss chard or collard greens instead of spinach. Just cook the lasagna a little longer. Fresh lasagna sheets can be used as well.

Per serving: Calories: 564; Fat: 14g; Protein: 25g; Carbohydrates: 93g; Fiber: 11g; Sodium: 184mg

SPAGHETTI SQUASH WITH VEGAN BOLOGNESE

DAIRY-FREE • GLUTEN-FREE • NUT-FREE • VEGAN
Prep time: 5 minutes • **Cook time:** 30 minutes
Yield: 2 to 4 servings

While traditional spaghetti is a treat, I also love preparing my favorite pasta dishes with a grain-free, low-carbohydrate alternative such as zucchini noodles or spaghetti squash. I prefer zucchini noodles with turkey Bolognese, but for this vegan version, I love spaghetti squash. The shiitake mushrooms here add the perfect chewiness, and the tomatoes tie in nicely with the sweetness of the squash.

1 spaghetti squash, seeded, halved
1 tablespoon extra-virgin olive oil
1 small yellow onion, chopped
1 (13-ounce) can whole peeled tomatoes with juice, chopped
1 cup shitake mushrooms, chopped
2 tablespoons soybean meal (see Substitution tip)
¾ teaspoon Himalayan salt
1 cup water
Freshly ground black pepper (optional)

Spice it up!
¼ teaspoon garlic
½ teaspoon basil
1 teaspoon parsley

1. Preheat the oven to 425°F. Put the spaghetti squash on a baking sheet, cut-side down. Bake until tender, about 30 minutes.
2. Meanwhile, in a small, nonstick sauté pan or skillet, heat the olive oil. Add the onions and garlic (if using). Cook for 2 minutes. Add the mushrooms, soybean meal, salt, basil (if using), tomatoes and juice from the can. Stir and add the water. Cover, reduce heat to low, and cook for about 30 minutes.

3. When the squash is baked, use a fork to scrape out the squash in spaghetti-like strands into a bowl.
4. Add the sauce over the spaghetti squash. Top with some black pepper and fresh parsley or basil, if desired. Enjoy warm.

* **Substitution tip:** You can use steel-cut oats instead of the soybean meal. Just add an extra 1 to 2 tablespoons of water, as the oats will soak up more. The squash can also be replaced with zucchini noodles or regular spaghetti.

Per serving: Calories: 189; Fat: 9g; Protein: 5g; Carbohydrates: 28g; Fiber: 8g; Sodium: 472mg

Grass-Fed Sirloin
Steak with Chimichurri
page 134

CHAPTER SEVEN

POULTRY AND MEAT

This chapter will focus on some simple ways to prepare delicious meat-based main meals. Many of these clean recipes are healthier versions of dishes you may know that are made with a lot of butter, deep-fried, or both. For example, you will love the Baked Chicken Tenders recipe—the chicken is perfectly crispy on the outside and juicy on the inside. It sure tastes fried, but because it's baked, it's so much better for us. In addition to chicken dishes, you'll also find mains featuring turkey, veal, and grass-fed beef dishes. You'll have fun combining these main dishes with some of the wonderful soups or salads from chapter 3, or rice or quinoa dishes from chapter 5.

Grilled Turkey Breast Marinated in Yogurt 124

Turkey Bolognese 125

Mexican-Inspired Turkey Burgers 126

Unstuffed Stuffed Peppers 127

Lemon Chicken with Capers 128

Greek-Style Grilled Chicken 129

Baked Chicken Tenders 130

Braised Cabbage with Chicken 131

Veal Cutlets in Green Pepper Sauce 132

Veal Goulash 133

＊ Grass-Fed Sirloin Steak with Chimichurri 134

Beef Burgers Stuffed with Feta and Prosciutto 135

GRILLED TURKEY BREAST MARINATED IN YOGURT

GLUTEN-FREE • SOY-FREE • NUT-FREE

Prep time: 30 minutes • **Cook time:** 15 minutes
Yield: 4 to 6 servings

What's the trick to juicy chicken and turkey meat? Marinating them in yogurt! You won't be able to taste the yogurt, just the perfectly juicy meat. The marinade in this recipe uses cumin, turmeric, and garlic, but you can add any spices you like, including fresh herbs. For example, fresh oregano, mint, lemon, and garlic are all wonderful, too. The longer you marinate the chicken, the nicer the flavor will be. I sometimes even leave it in the marinade overnight. Once you take the meat out of the marinade, drain it in a colander, then proceed with grilling it.

2 pounds turkey breast, cubed
Greek Yogurt Marinade (page 162)

1. Preheat the grill while you are marinating the turkey. (See Substitution tip for stovetop cooking.)
2. Add cubed turkey to the yogurt and stir until everything is coated evenly. Leave it in the marinade for at least 30 minutes.
3. When turkey is marinated, drain the marinade and slide the meat onto the skewers.
4. Grill the meat as you usually do.

✳ **Prep tip:** Considering that the turkey was marinated in lemon and yogurt, the cooking time should be shorter than usual. Lemon partially cooks the meat while in the marinade.

✳ **Substitution tip:** If you don't have a grill, simply cook the turkey in a greased cast-iron pan over medium-high heat. You can also use chicken instead of turkey.

Per serving: Calories: 310; Fat: 10g; Protein: 54g; Carbohydrates: 2g; Fiber: 0g; Sodium: 211mg

TURKEY BOLOGNESE

DAIRY-FREE • GLUTEN-FREE • NUT-FREE • SOY-FREE
Prep time: 5 minutes • **Cook time:** 25 minutes
Yield: 6 servings

Pasta Bolognese is traditionally made with ground beef or pork. Bacon is also added, as well as some milk or cream to make the meat softer. While that version is really delicious, it is quite heavy on the digestion system. Once in a while, a small portion is fine, of course. You wouldn't want to be in Rome and miss out on tasting delicious pastas made by Italians, that's for sure! This clean version of pasta Bolognese is dairy-free, made with turkey, and omits the bacon. I suggest serving it with zucchini noodles, whole-grain pasta, or brown rice.

2 tablespoons extra-virgin olive oil
1 yellow onion, chopped
1 garlic clove, minced
2 pounds ground turkey
34 ounces tomato puree or juice
1½ teaspoons Himalayan salt
1 teaspoon oregano

1. In a saucepan over medium heat, heat the olive oil. Add the onion and garlic, and sauté until the onion is translucent.
2. Add the turkey and sauté until the turkey turns white.
3. Add the tomato puree, salt, and oregano.
4. Cover, reduce heat to low, and simmer for about 30 minutes.
5. Serve warm over your choice of pasta, rice, or zoodles.

* **Storage tip:** Bolognese is one of those great dishes that can last in the refrigerator for a full week if stored in a glass container.

* **Substitution tip:** You can replace the oregano with basil. You can also use fresh oregano or basil; just chop a few leaves and add them to the sauce as directed.

Per serving: Calories: 301; Fat: 17g; Protein: 30g; Carbohydrates: 8g; Fiber: 3g; Sodium: 427mg

MEXICAN-INSPIRED TURKEY BURGERS

DAIRY-FREE · GLUTEN-FREE · NUT-FREE · SOY-FREE

Prep time: 5 minutes · **Cook time:** 45 minutes
Yield: 12 mini burgers

Turkey meat dries out fast, so when making burgers from ground turkey, some doctoring up is needed. Adding onion always does the trick, as well as an egg or some warm water. In this recipe I added peppers, which naturally contain a lot of water and add moisture to the mixture. Mexican-inspired spices such as cumin and chili powder add so much flavor that if you choose to use them, all you'll need to add is a simple bun or butter lettuce leaves.

1⅓ pounds ground turkey
½ yellow onion, finely diced
1 green pepper, finely diced
1 teaspoon Himalayan salt
1 large egg, beaten
2 tablespoons extra-virgin olive oil

Spice it up!
1 teaspoon cumin
1 teaspoon chili powder

1. Preheat a grill to the highest setting. (See Substitution tip for stovetop directions.)
2. In a large bowl, combine the turkey, onion, pepper, cumin and chili powder (if using), and salt. Mix well until combined.
3. Add the egg and mix again.
4. Form 12 small turkey patties and set them on a plate. Rub each patty with olive oil, cover with plastic, and refrigerate for about 30 minutes.
5. Grill until cooked through.

* **Prep tip:** You can make these ahead of time and store covered in the refrigerator overnight.

* **Substitution tip:** If you don't have a grill, you can make these burgers in an oiled cast-iron skillet over medium-high heat. You can also make these burgers egg-free: Just add ⅛ cup warm water instead.

Per serving (2 burgers): Calories: 210; Fat: 14g; Protein: 20g; Carbohydrates: 2g; Fiber: 1g; Sodium: 276mg

UNSTUFFED STUFFED PEPPERS

DAIRY-FREE • GLUTEN-FREE • NUT-FREE • SOY-FREE
Prep time: 5 minutes • **Cook time:** 30 minutes
Yield: 4 servings

My husband came home from the grocery store one day with a few frozen meals. Usually we do not buy frozen meals, but he said one seemed interesting because it contained stuffed peppers, and had oats in it, too. I looked at the ingredients and was pleased to see that the frozen meal was made from "real" ingredients. I decided to try and "copy" the dish and voilà! This recipe was born!

2 tablespoons extra-virgin olive oil
1 yellow onion, diced
2 garlic cloves, minced
3 bell peppers, diced
1 pound ground turkey
2 teaspoons Himalayan salt
3 cups tomato purée
1 cup water
⅓ cup steel-cut oats, uncooked

Spice it up!
1 teaspoon oregano
1 teaspoon basil
1 teaspoon garlic powder

1. In a saucepan over medium heat, heat the olive oil. Add the onion, garlic, and peppers. Sauté until the onion is translucent.
2. Add the ground turkey, then the oregano, basil, garlic powder (if using), and salt. Stir and cook for about 1 minute.
3. Add the tomato puree, water, and oats. Cover, reduce heat to low, and cook for about 30 minutes, uncovering to stir occasionally so oats don't stick to the bottom.
4. Uncover, stir, and cook for 5 more minutes.
5. Serve warm.

✳ **Ingredient tip:** I usually use 3 different colors of peppers: yellow, red, and green.

Per serving: Calories: 349; Fat: 17g; Protein: 25g; Carbohydrates: 25g; Fiber: 6g; Sodium: 852mg

LEMON CHICKEN WITH CAPERS

DAIRY-FREE • GLUTEN-FREE • NUT-FREE • SOY-FREE

Prep time: 5 minutes • **Cook time:** 20 minutes
Yield: 4 servings

This is one of the easiest and tastiest chicken recipes you can make. The dish is very light, but suitable in all seasons. During the warmer months, serve it with grilled veggies or over arugula, and during the winter, serve it with braised cabbage or oven-baked potatoes. This recipe traditionally uses white flour for dusting the meat, but I use almond, because it's healthier and I like the nutty flavor it adds.

---

3 tablespoons almond flour
1 pound boneless, skinless chicken breast, thinly sliced
½ teaspoon Himalayan salt
2 tablespoons extra-virgin olive oil
Juice of 1 large lemon
2 tablespoons capers
¼ cup water
Freshly ground black pepper (optional)
1 tablespoon fresh oregano, chopped (optional)

1. Pour the almond flour on a shallow plate. Set aside.
2. Pound the chicken on both sides, sprinkle with salt, and dip each side into the almond flour. Pat off the extra flour.
3. In a large, nonstick sauté pan or skillet over medium heat, heat the olive oil.
4. Add the chicken and cook on one side for about 3 minutes, then flip. Cover and cook for about 2 minutes, then squeeze lemon all over the chicken, and add the capers and ¼ cup water. Cover and reduce heat to low.
5. When the water evaporates, flip the meat once again, cook for 1 minute, and remove from heat.
6. If desired, squeeze extra lemon juice on top as well as some freshly ground black pepper. Add fresh oregano as a finishing touch (if using).

* **Substitution tip:** You can use turkey breast or veal instead of chicken, but a longer cooking time will be required. After your first addition of lemon, water, and capers evaporates, add another ¼ cup water. Cover and proceed as directed. You can also replace the almond flour with any flour of your choice.

Per serving: Calories: 227; Fat: 12g; Protein: 27g; Carbohydrates: 2g; Fiber: 1g; Sodium: 298mg

GREEK-STYLE GRILLED CHICKEN

GLUTEN-FREE • NUT-FREE • SOY-FREE

Prep time: 5 minutes • **Cook time:** 25 minutes
Yield: 4 to 6 servings

Grilling season is the perfect opportunity to enjoy freshly grilled veggies and lean cuts of meat and seafood. A few years ago, my husband made this grilled chicken for us, and ever since then it has been on repeat in our household. The chicken comes out perfectly tender, with hints of lemon and garlic as an aftertaste. You can make this dish with cutlets or cut the chicken in cubes and make chicken skewers. This is a good idea if you're having a barbecue party, because skewers are much easier to pass around and hold.

4 boneless, skinless chicken breasts, halved lengthwise
Kefir Marinade (page 163)
Olive oil for basting

1. Preheat the grill on highest setting. (See Substitution tip for stovetop option.)
2. Pour the marinade into a large bowl.
3. Add sliced chicken cutlets and mix well.
4. Let marinate for at least 30 minutes.
5. Using a colander, drain the chicken.
6. Baste the chicken once the grill has warmed up and grill it as you usually would.

* **Substitution tip:** This chicken can also be cooked in an oiled cast-iron skillet over medium-high heat.

* **Prep tip:** The longer you marinate the chicken, the juicer it will be when grilled.

Per serving: Calories: 166; Fat: 6g; Protein: 25g; Carbohydrates: 0g; Fiber: 0g; Sodium: 51mg

BAKED CHICKEN TENDERS

DAIRY-FREE · GLUTEN-FREE · NUT-FREE · SOY-FREE
Prep time: 5 minutes · **Cook time:** 30 minutes
Yield: 4 to 6 servings

Want perfectly crispy but juicy chicken tenders? There is no need to deep-fry them or even invest in an expensive air fryer. All you need is some mustard, a good breading mixture, a drizzle of olive oil, and a hot oven. Mustard is truly a secret ingredient here because it keeps the chicken tender and prevents it from drying out. You can use this little trick with any meat, especially if you are grilling it. Once you bake or grill the meat, you cannot taste the mustard, so even if you're not a mustard lover, you will enjoy this recipe.

4 boneless, skinless chicken breasts, washed and cut into tenders
½ teaspoon Himalayan salt
1 tablespoon Dijon mustard
½ cup spelt flour
2 large eggs, beaten
¾ cup gluten-free bread crumbs
1 tablespoon extra-virgin olive oil or olive oil spray

Spice it up!
1 teaspoon oregano

1. Preheat the oven to 400°F. Line a baking sheet with parchment paper and set aside.
2. Pat the chicken dry with a paper towel. Rub all over with the salt and mustard.
3. Pour the flour in one shallow dish, the eggs in another, and the bread crumbs in a third. Dip both sides of each tender into the flour, then the eggs, then the bread crumbs, finally placing them on the baking sheet.
4. Sprinkle oregano on top of each of the tenders, if desired, then drizzle or spray olive oil on top.
5. Bake for about 30 minutes, flipping once halfway through cook time.
6. Serve warm.

✳ **Storage tip:** These chicken tenders hold up well stored in a glass container in the refrigerator. The next day, warm them up in the oven or microwave, or enjoy them cold over a salad.

Per serving: Calories: 339; Fat: 10g; Protein: 34g; Carbohydrates: 26g; Fiber: 1g; Sodium: 439mg

BRAISED CABBAGE WITH CHICKEN

GLUTEN-FREE • NUT-FREE • SOY-FREE
Prep time: 5 minutes · **Cook time:** 45 minutes
Yield: 4 servings

Cabbage can truly be called a "superfood." (See page 5 to learn about its benefits.) That said, it's good to find versatile ways to use cabbage. Next to soups and stews, cabbage is also wonderful pickled or raw in salads. One of my favorite salads in warmer months is shredded cabbage with olive oil, lemon, and salt. But for a warming, healing fall and winter dish, this braised cabbage really hits the spot.

2 tablespoons extra-virgin olive oil
1 yellow onion, chopped
3 carrots, cubed
1 pound boneless, skinless chicken breasts, diced
2 teaspoons Himalayan salt
1 large cabbage, coarsely chopped into big chunks
6 cups water
1 large potato, diced

Spice it up!
¼ teaspoon garlic powder
1 teaspoon red paprika

1. In a large stockpot, heat the olive oil over medium heat. Add the onion, carrots, and garlic powder (if using). Sauté until the onion is translucent, about 3 minutes.
2. Add the diced chicken, salt, and paprika (if using). Sauté until the chicken is white on all sides.
3. Add the cabbage and water. Stir to combine, cover, reduce heat to low, and cook for about 20 minutes.
4. Add the potatoes, cover again, and cook for about 10 minutes, then uncover and cook for 10 more minutes to evaporate the water and thicken the stew.

* **Substitution tip:** You can use turkey or veal in this recipe as well. Because the meat is diced small, cooking time will be about the same.

Per serving: Calories: 375; Fat: 10g; Protein: 32g; Carbohydrates: 41g; Fiber: 12g; Sodium: 872mg

VEAL CUTLETS IN GREEN PEPPER SAUCE

GLUTEN-FREE • **NUT-FREE** • **SOY-FREE**

Prep time: 5 minutes • **Cook time:** 30 minutes
Yield: 3 to 4 servings

In Serbia, this is a pretty common way to prepare veal or pork. The original recipe is a bit different, as it involves flouring the meat, but the end taste is almost the same. Dijon mustard prevents the meat from drying out, and at the same time, it adds a lot of flavor, as does the green pepper. I love serving this with brown or basmati rice or over mashed potatoes.

3 tablespoons extra-virgin olive oil
6 veal cutlets (about 1⅓ pounds)
1 long green Cubanelle pepper, chopped
3 garlic cloves, minced
2 tablespoons Dijon mustard
½ teaspoon Himalayan salt
Freshly ground black pepper (optional)

1. In a large, nonstick sauté pan or skillet over medium heat, heat the olive oil. Working in batches if needed, add the veal piece by piece. Brown on both sides, then transfer to a plate and set aside.
2. In the same pan, add the chopped peppers and garlic. Cook for about 2 minutes, then add the veal back in, overlapping if necessary.
3. Add ¼ cup water, cover, reduce heat to low, and cook until the water evaporates, 5 to 6 minutes. Repeat this step 2 more times, until the veal is soft under the fork.
4. Add some black pepper, if desired, and serve warm.

✳ **Substitution tip:** You can use yellow mustard instead of Dijon. Chicken or turkey breast, thinly sliced, can be used instead of veal.

Per serving: Calories: 357; Fat: 19g; Protein: 42g; Carbohydrates: 3g; Fiber: 1g; Sodium: 471mg

VEAL GOULASH

DAIRY-FREE • GLUTEN-FREE • NUT-FREE • SOY-FREE
Prep time: 5 minutes • **Cook time:** 50 minutes
Yield: 4 servings

Traditional goulash is made with pork or beef and cooked on low heat for a couple of hours. Veal is a much softer meat, so it cooks faster; that's why I decided to use it in this recipe. It delivers the same great taste, but with less time spent in the kitchen making it. Typically, goulash is served over mashed potatoes or plain spaghetti, but I also love it over zoodles or brown rice.

2 tablespoons extra-virgin olive oil
1 yellow onion, chopped
1 small carrot, grated
1¾ pounds veal, cut into small cubes
1 teaspoon Himalayan salt
½ cup red cooking wine
13 ounces tomato puree
1½ to 2 cups water, divided

Spice it up!
1 teaspoon red paprika

1. In a large sauté pan or skillet over medium heat, heat the olive oil. Add the onion, garlic, and carrots. Sauté until the onion is translucent.
2. Add the veal and cook, turning, until the meat is brown on all sides. Add the salt and paprika (if using).
3. Add the wine and 1 cup of water. Cover, reduce heat to low, and cook for 25 minutes, until most of the liquid evaporates.
4. Add the tomato puree and 1½ cups of water. Cover and cook for another 25 minutes.
5. Check if the meat is tender and falling apart. If so, remove from heat. If the meat is not as soft as you would like, add another ½ cup of water and cook for another 10 minutes.

✳ **Prep tip:** Depending how high the heat is, the liquid may evaporate before the meat is cooked. If that happens, just add some more water, cover, and continue cooking.

✳ **Substitution tip:** You can use low-sodium vegetable or chicken stock instead of water.

Per serving: Calories: 359; Fat: 12g; Protein: 41g; Carbohydrates: 9g; Fiber: 3g; Sodium: 471mg

GRASS-FED SIRLOIN STEAK WITH CHIMICHURRI

DAIRY-FREE · GLUTEN-FREE · NUT-FREE · SOY-FREE
Prep time: 5 minutes, plus 15 minutes to stand · **Cook time:** 15 minutes
Yield: 4 servings

If there's one recipe in this cookbook that looks like a restaurant-style meal, it's this one. The quality of the meat in this recipe is important—but no matter what cut you choose, the marinade is what really takes this dish to the next level. I suggest you try this with grass-fed sirloin steak or filet mignon. But I also love this marinade with veal chops or over beef brisket. The steak is wonderful when served with roasted potatoes, or over cauliflower, mashed potatoes, or simple grilled vegetables.

4 (6-ounce) grass-fed sirloin steaks
1 tablespoon extra-virgin olive oil
½ teaspoon Himalayan salt
½ batch Chimichurri Sauce (page 159)

1. Preheat the grill at the highest setting. (See Substitution tip for stovetop option.)
2. Rub the steaks with the olive oil and sprinkle with salt. Let the steak stand at room temperature for about 15 minutes.
3. Grill the steaks to your preferred doneness. Let rest for about 5 minutes before adding to plates.
4. Enjoy warm with some chimichurri on top.

* **Substitution tip:** You can also cook these steaks in a hot, oiled cast-iron skillet.

* **Prep tip:** You can also slice the grilled steaks thin, arrange them on a platter, and then add the sauce on top. Steak like this can also be refrigerated and served cold over salad the next day.

Per serving: Calories: 494; Fat: 38g; Protein: 35g; Carbohydrates: 0g; Fiber: 0g; Sodium: 270mg

BEEF BURGERS STUFFED WITH FETA AND PROSCIUTTO

GLUTEN-FREE • NUT-FREE • SOY-FREE
Prep time: 5 minutes • **Cook time:** 15 minutes
Yield: 4 (6-ounce) burgers

For any type of red meat, it is important to focus on quality rather than quantity. Large industry-grown animals are often kept enclosed, mistreated, and given antibiotics. Those antibiotics are passed onto us and they can cause health problems down the road. Buying organic, grass-fed, or pasture-raised meat is more expensive, but it is healthier. Supporting your small, local farm is a good place to start.

2 ounces feta, crumbled
3 ounces prosciutto, diced
1½ pounds ground, grass-fed beef
1 small yellow onion, finely diced
½ teaspoon Himalayan salt
1 tablespoon extra-virgin olive oil, for brushing the grill

Spice it up!
½ teaspoon garlic powder

1. Preheat the grill to the highest setting. (See Substitution tip for stovetop option.)
2. Divide the feta and prosciutto into 4 equal parts. Set aside.
3. In a large bowl, combine the ground beef, onion, salt, and garlic powder (if using). Mix well.
4. Split the meat into 8 parts. Shape each portion into a patty.
5. Add the feta and prosciutto to the middle of 4 patties. Put the remaining 4 patties on top of the first patties, and close off the edges by pressing the sides of the burgers together.
6. Brush the grill with olive oil, and grill the burgers, flipping occasionally, until cooked to desired doneness.
7. Serve warm on whole-grain buns or over lettuce.

* **Prep tip:** You can dip the formed patties into coarse polenta for more texture.

* **Substitution tip:** You can use shallots instead of yellow onion. Cow milk feta or vegan feta can be used instead of regular feta.

Per serving: Calories: 349; Fat: 18g; Protein: 43g; Carbohydrates: 2g; Fiber: 0g; Sodium: 857mg

Shrimp Tacos with Mango Salsa
page 146

CHAPTER EIGHT

FISH AND SEAFOOD

Wild-caught fish and seafood are among the most nutrient-dense, flavorful protein sources available. The idea behind this chapter is to make fish and seafood dishes less intimidating. These recipes consist of only 5 main ingredients, they take only a few minutes to prepare, and cooking time is minimal, making this a great place to try cooking fish and seafood. From Tuna Burgers and Baked Cod Fillets in Mushroom Sauce to Shrimp Saganaki and Miso-Glazed Salmon, these clean recipes will be a great addition to your healthy eating lifestyle. No longer must you rely on restaurants to provide you with your favorite seafood dishes!

Grilled Ahi Tuna **138**

Tuna Burgers **139**

Tuna Salad **140**

Baked Cod Fillets in Mushroom Sauce **141**

Codfish Risotto with Saffron **142**

Shrimp with Zoodles **143**

Shrimp Saganaki **144**

＊ Shrimp Tacos with Mango Salsa **146**

Roasted Branzino with Lemon Potatoes **147**

Miso-Glazed Salmon **148**

Baked Salmon with Parmesan Asparagus **149**

Seared Scallops **150**

GRILLED AHI TUNA

DAIRY-FREE • GLUTEN-FREE • NUT-FREE
Prep time: 15 minutes • **Cook time:** 5 minutes
Yield: 2 servings

When eating raw or seared fish like tuna, it is important to pick the good-quality kind. Uncooked fish can cause food poisoning. There is less danger when the fish is cooked through, as the bacteria are killed under high heat. When you are at the fish market or a grocery store, inquire about the origin of the fish, how fresh it is, and whether it is sushi grade. If you are pregnant, it's best to avoid anything that is not fully cooked, just to be safe. Enjoy this light protein along with a nice green salad.

FOR THE MARINADE
2 tablespoons soy sauce
1 tablespoon sesame oil
1 tablespoon rice vinegar

FOR THE TUNA
2 (6-ounce) ahi tuna steaks
Sesame seeds (optional)

1. Preheat the grill to the highest setting. (See Substitution tip for stovetop option.)
2. **To make the marinade:** In a small bowl, whisk together the soy sauce, sesame oil, and rice vinegar.
3. **To make the tuna:** Wash the tuna steaks and pat them dry. Add the steaks to a bowl, and pour the marinade on top. Rub the steaks on both sides to coat evenly. Leave at room temperature for about 15 minutes.
4. Grill the steaks for 3 minutes on one side and 2 minutes on the other. The steaks will be seared on the outside and pink on the inside.
5. Slice thin and serve alongside a large green salad of your choice. Sprinkle some sesame seeds on top, if desired.

✳ **Substitution tip:** If you don't have a grill, you can cook these steaks in a hot, oiled cast-iron skillet. You can also use coconut aminos instead of soy sauce.

Per serving: Calories: 256; Fat: 8g; Protein: 43g; Carbohydrates: 1g; Fiber: 0g; Sodium: 455mg

TUNA BURGERS

DAIRY-FREE · GLUTEN-FREE · NUT-FREE · SOY-FREE

Prep time: 5 minutes · **Cook time:** 10 minutes

Yield: 2 to 4 servings

These tuna burgers remind me of a really good tuna salad, just in burger form. I suggest trying these with butter or romaine lettuce as buns, but you can also use toasted whole-grain bread. I also like to add some shredded cabbage and tartar sauce on top. Such a great combination of flavors! When buying canned tuna, look for skipjack—it's the lowest in mercury. Also, look for the tuna in water and not oil. If it's in oil, make sure it's in olive oil.

1 (8½-ounce can) tuna in water, drained

1 tablespoon Dijon mustard

1 scallion, chopped (green and white parts)

½ cup baby spinach, chopped

½ cup cornmeal (polenta)

½ teaspoon Himalayan salt

¼ teaspoon freshly ground black pepper

2 tablespoons extra-virgin olive oil

1. In a small bowl, combine the tuna, mustard, scallion, spinach, cornmeal, salt, and pepper. Mix well.
2. Form 2 large or 4 small patties. Set aside.
3. In a nonstick sauté pan or skillet over medium heat, heat the olive oil. Add the burgers and panfry on one side for 3 to 4 minutes, then flip and leave them for another 3 minutes.
4. Transfer the burgers onto a plate lined with a paper towel to soak up some of the excess olive oil.

✳ **Substitution tip:** You can use oat flour instead of corn meal.

Per serving: Calories: 319; Fat: 16g; Protein: 22g; Carbohydrates: 24g; Fiber: 3g; Sodium: 510mg

TUNA SALAD

DAIRY-FREE · GLUTEN-FREE · NUT-FREE · SOY-FREE

Prep time: 5 minutes
Yield: 2 servings

Tuna is something I always keep stocked in the pantry. It really comes in handy on busy nights. Sometimes, all it takes is opening a can of tuna and topping your favorite salad greens with it. And if you have a tuna salad already prepared, endless options abound for a delicious lunch or dinner. I suggest using tuna, scallions (or onions or shallots), and Dijon as a base, and then adding any fresh veggies that you like. Some of my favorites are celery, shredded cabbage, carrots, and shredded Brussels sprouts.

1 (8½-ounce) can tuna packed in olive oil
⅓ cup shredded carrots
⅓ cup parsley, chopped
2 scallions, chopped (green and white parts)
1 tablespoon Dijon mustard
¼ teaspoon Himalayan salt
Whole-grain toast (optional)
Avocado slices (optional)

1. In a medium bowl, combine the tuna with all the oil from the can, carrots, parsley, scallions, Dijon mustard, and salt. Mix well.
2. Serve over whole-grain toast with avocado slices on top, if desired.

❋ **Serving tip:** This tuna salad is great on whole-grain or sourdough toast, on high-fiber crackers, or on a bed of arugula with some cherry tomatoes, olive oil, and lemon. It is also wonderful for a yummy tuna melt for the coziest nights.

Per serving: Calories: 205; Fat: 8g; Protein: 27g; Carbohydrates: 4g; Fiber: 2g; Sodium: 315mg

BAKED COD FILLETS IN MUSHROOM SAUCE

DAIRY-FREE • GLUTEN-FREE • NUT-FREE • SOY-FREE
Prep time: 5 minutes • **Cook time:** 25 minutes
Yield: 2 servings

This dish is inspired by a dish I had in Greece. I loved the balance the chef struck between the simple fish and the complexity of the tomato sauce with veggies. The restaurant version was made with white button mushrooms and black olives. Here I use shiitake mushrooms because of their chewy texture. This fish is wonderful served over brown rice with capers and fresh oregano on top.

1 tablespoon extra-virgin olive oil, plus more for serving
1½ cups shiitake mushrooms, chopped
2 garlic cloves, minced
½ teaspoon Himalayan salt
¾ cup crushed tomatoes
1 tablespoon fresh oregano, chopped
2 codfish fillets, washed and patted dry
Freshly ground black pepper

1. Preheat the oven to 400°F. Line a small baking sheet with parchment paper and set aside.
2. In a small, nonstick sauté pan or skillet over medium heat, heat the olive oil. Add the shiitake mushrooms and sauté for 2 minutes, then add the garlic and salt.
3. Add the crushed tomatoes and continue cooking for 5 minutes, until the sauce is reduced by one-third. Stir in the oregano.
4. Put the cod fillets on the prepared baking sheet and spoon some of the mushroom tomato mixture over each. Add any leftover sauce to the baking sheet.
5. Bake for about 20 minutes, until fish is cooked through.
6. Add some black pepper and a drizzle of olive oil before serving.

✳ **Prep tip:** If you like things spicy, you can add red pepper flakes to the mushroom sauce before placing it in the oven. Also, sometimes canned tomatoes can be a little acidic, so you can add a pinch of sugar to the sauce.

✳ **Substitution tip:** Use any type of white fish for this dish. The flakier the fish, the better.

Per serving: Calories: 209; Fat: 8g; Protein: 28g; Carbohydrates: 6g; Fiber: 3g; Sodium: 518mg

CODFISH RISOTTO WITH SAFFRON

DAIRY-FREE · GLUTEN-FREE · NUT-FREE · SOY-FREE
Prep time: 5 minutes · **Cook time:** 20 minutes
Yield: 4 servings

This recipe is fairly simple to put together and yet seems so complex when done. There is no cream or any dairy in this recipe—the creaminess simply comes from cooking on low heat with olive oil. I used cod, but feel free to use any kind of white fish fillet. Even thin fillets like tilapia work. It's important to use arborio (risotto) rice in this dish, though, because it cooks differently from white rice.

2 tablespoons extra-virgin olive oil
2 leeks, white parts only, thinly sliced (optional)
½ medium yellow onion, thinly sliced
2 garlic cloves, minced
1 cup arborio rice, washed and drained
½ teaspoon Himalayan salt
¼ teaspoon saffron
1 pound codfish fillets, washed and patted dry, cut into small rectangles
2 cups water
Freshly ground black pepper (optional)

1. In a large sauté pan or skillet over medium heat, heat the olive oil. Add the leeks, onion, and garlic. Sauté until the onion is translucent.
2. Add the rice, salt, and saffron. Stir to combine.
3. Make small pockets in the rice and insert the fish.
4. Add the water, cover, reduce heat to low, and cook for 20 minutes. Most of the liquid will evaporate.
5. Add some more saffron and black pepper, if desired. Serve warm.

* **Substitution tip:** Saffron is expensive, so you can use ¼ teaspoon of turmeric instead.

Per serving: Calories: 513; Fat: 11g; Protein: 32g; Carbohydrates: 68g; Fiber: 4g; Sodium: 353mg

SHRIMP WITH ZOODLES

GLUTEN-FREE • NUT-FREE • SOY-FREE
Prep time: 5 min • **Cook time:** 25 min
Yield: 2 to 3

When buying marinara sauce, opt for glass-jarred sauces made with real food ingredients. Check to be sure there is little or no sugar or high-fructose corn syrup. Typically, the ingredients you'll want to see in marinara sauce are tomatoes, onions, carrots, celery, garlic, oregano, basil, and salt.

1 pound shrimp, cleaned
1 tablespoon extra-virgin olive oil
Juice of ½ lemon
½ cup marinara sauce
4 medium green zucchini, spiralized
1 tablespoon freshly grated Parmesan cheese

Spice it up!
¼ teaspoon garlic powder
Red pepper flakes, for garnishing

1. Preheat the grill to the highest setting. Baste with olive oil if needed.
2. In a bowl, toss the shrimp with the olive oil, garlic powder (if using), and lemon juice. Marinate for about 10 minutes.
3. Grill the shrimp on one side for 3 minutes, then flip and cook for another 3 minutes. Remove from heat and set aside.
4. In a small sauté pan or skillet, bring the marinara sauce to a boil. Add the spiralized zucchini and sauté for about 3 minutes, until tender. Sprinkle with the Parmesan cheese, toss, and remove from the heat.
5. Serve zoodles on individual plates with shrimp on top. Add red pepper flakes if you like it spicy.

✳ **Prep tip:** Once you spiralize zucchini, you can wrap it in a paper towel and store it in the refrigerator overnight. The next day, proceed as outlined in the recipe.

✳ **Serving tip:** You can add oregano and basil to the sauce, if you wish.

✳ **Ingredient tip:** Once you spiralize the zucchini, it's important to drain it well. Wrap the zucchini noodles in a triple layer of paper towels. Leave them in a colander for about 15 minutes.

Per serving: Calories: 315; Fat: 11g; Protein: 37g; Carbohydrates: 19g; Fiber: 5g; Sodium: 353mg

SHRIMP SAGANAKI

GLUTEN-FREE • NUT-FREE • SOY-FREE
Prep time: 15 min • **Cook time:** 30 min
Yield: 2

Shrimp Saganaki is a signature dish that my husband likes to make for us often. I've been watching him make this dish for a long time now, and realized that although he changes up the herbs and spices from time to time, the base of this recipe always stays the same: shrimp, whole peeled tomatoes, garlic, olive oil, and feta cheese. Splashing a little whiskey over the shrimp is his secret step, which I omitted for the purposes of this cookbook, but you can certainly add it from time to time if you're feeling adventurous. I recommend baking this in a clay baking dish if you have one—it makes a difference.

1 pound shrimp, cleaned
3 garlic cloves, chopped
1 tablespoon extra-virgin olive oil
1 (13-ounce) can whole peeled tomatoes (with liquid), mashed or chopped small
1 (13-ounce) can tomato puree
1 tablespoon fresh basil, chopped
½ teaspoon oregano
½ teaspoon Himalayan salt
2 or 3 tablespoons feta
Freshly ground black pepper (optional)

1. In a bowl, combine the shrimp, garlic, and olive oil. Stir and marinate for at least 15 minutes.
2. In another bowl, add the tomatoes, tomato puree, basil, oregano, and salt. Mix and set aside.
3. Preheat the oven to 425°F.
4. Heat a cast-iron skillet over high heat. When the skillet is very hot, toss in the shrimp. Flash-fry for about 3 minutes on each side, leaving the shrimp half cooked, just until they turn pink.
5. Transfer the shrimp to a baking dish, then add the tomato mixture. Sprinkle feta on top and add black pepper, if desired.
6. Bake until the cheese is bubbly, 10 to 15 minutes.
7. Serve warm by itself or over some jasmine or brown rice.

* **Prep tip:** It is important that the skillet is really hot so the shrimp panfries as opposed to cooking. If the pan is not hot enough, the shrimp will release its water. Do not be afraid of a little smoke—just use caution.

* **Substitution tip:** You can use ½ teaspoon dry basil instead of fresh. Fresh plum tomatoes can also be used when in season. Just add the tomatoes to boiling water, and remove from heat once the skin cracks. Peel the skin off and chop the tomatoes. Proceed with the recipe as directed.

Per serving: Calories: 359; Fat: 12g; Protein: 51g; Carbohydrates: 15g; Fiber: 7g; Sodium: 512mg

SHRIMP TACOS WITH MANGO SALSA

DAIRY-FREE · GLUTEN-FREE · NUT-FREE · SOY-FREE
Prep time: 20 minutes · **Cook time:** 10 minutes
Yield: 2 servings

While tomato-based salsa is fresh and delicious, there is something about mango salsa and its combination with seafood that speaks volumes. The sweetness of the mango balances, and the freshness of herbs and the spiciness of onions counterbalance, the simplicity of the seafood, whether it is shrimp, squid, or sea bass. I suggest that you start with this recipe, then explore using mango salsa with grilled squid or oven-baked sea bass.

1 pound shrimp, cleaned
Juice of ½ lemon
½ teaspoon Himalayan salt
1 tablespoon extra-virgin olive oil
Corn tortillas or butter lettuce leaves
Mango Salsa (page 160)

1. In a resealable bag, combine the shrimp, lemon juice, and salt. Mix and marinate for about 20 minutes.
2. In a cast-iron skillet over medium heat, heat the olive oil. Panfry the shrimp, flipping once, until cooked through, about 8 minutes total.
3. Add some shrimp to a tortilla or butter lettuce cup, add some mango salsa on top, and enjoy warm.

* **Substitution tips:** To make this dish vegan, you can use pan-seared tofu instead of shrimp. If you prefer cilantro over parsley, that can be used as well.

Per serving: Calories: 281; Fat: 4g; Protein: 47g; Carbohydrates: 15g; Fiber: 2g; Sodium: 601mg

ROASTED BRANZINO WITH LEMON POTATOES

DAIRY-FREE • GLUTEN-FREE • NUT-FREE • SOY-FREE

Prep time: 5 minutes · **Cook time:** 20 minutes
Yield: 2 to 3 servings

Preparing whole fish is really simple, especially if you bake it in the oven. Branzino, sea bream, and red snapper have a very mild, neutral taste, so whatever herbs or spices you choose to use will determine the way the fish tastes. I usually opt for salt, olive oil, and garlic. These three ingredients are not over-powering and they bring out the flavors of the fish really nicely.

1 (1- to 1½-pound) whole branzino fish, cleaned
2 lemons, divided
¾ teaspoon Himalayan salt, divided
2 garlic cloves, minced
3 tablespoons extra-virgin olive oil, divided
2 large white potatoes, quartered
¼ yellow onion, thinly sliced

1. Preheat the oven to 425°F. Line a baking dish with parchment paper and set aside.
2. Squeeze half a lemon where the fish is split apart, add ¼ teaspoon of salt, and put the minced garlic inside.
3. Rub 1 tablespoon of olive oil all over the fish and place it in the prepared baking dish.
4. Bake for 20 to 25 minutes, until the fish is cooked through.
5. Take it out of the oven and let the fish rest for at least 10 minutes.
6. Meanwhile, boil the potatoes until tender, then drain.
7. Cut the potatoes into bite-size pieces. Sprinkle with the remaining ½ teaspoon of salt.
8. In a glass serving bowl, add the potatoes and sliced onions. Whisk the 2 remaining tablespoons of olive oil and the juice of the remaining 1½ lemons and pour over the potatoes. Toss gently and serve alongside the fish.

* **Prep tip:** Let the fish cool for at least 10 minutes before de-boning it.

* **Ingredient tips:** When the fish is almost roasted, you can switch the oven to broil so the top of the fish crisps up. If you choose to use broil, watch the fish closely because it can burn easily.

Per serving: Calories: 441; Fat: 15g; Protein: 35g; Carbohydrates: 42g; Fiber: 6g; Sodium: 676mg

MISO-GLAZED SALMON

DAIRY-FREE • NUT-FREE
Prep time: 20 minutes · **Cook time:** 25 minutes
Yield: 5 servings

Salmon is one of the healthiest fish because of its high omega-3 content. These beneficial fats are shown to help fight inflammation and manage blood pressure and blood sugar levels. Omega-3 fats are also shown to have a positive effect on brain cells, slowing down aging and even possibly preventing Alzheimer's. This is one of my favorite ways to make salmon, and my kids love it, too. I suggest serving it with one of the wonderful rice or quinoa dishes from chapter 5.

5 salmon fillets (about 2 pounds)
Miso Glaze (page 161)
Sesame seeds (optional)

1. Preheat the oven to 400°F. Line a baking dish with parchment paper and set aside.
2. Put the salmon in a large resealable bag and pour the glaze inside. Mix and marinate for about 20 minutes.
3. Transfer the salmon onto the baking sheet and spoon over the marinade. Sprinkle with the sesame seeds (if using).
4. Bake for 12 to 15 minutes, or to your liking.
5. Serve warm.

* **Substitution tip:** You can use coconut aminos instead of soy sauce.

Per serving: Calories: 259; Fat: 12g; Protein: 37g; Carbohydrates: 5g; Fiber: 0g; Sodium: 520mg

BAKED SALMON WITH PARMESAN ASPARAGUS

GLUTEN-FREE • NUT-FREE • SOY-FREE

Prep time: 5 minutes • **Cook time:** 25 minutes
Yield: 4 servings

Asparagus is a veggie that is often forgotten, but which definitely deserves a place on our table. This lovely, dark-green veggie contains a good amount of iron and is rich in protein and fiber. Asparagus can be prepared many ways, and all of them are so simple; it takes only 10 minutes. This recipe involves roasting and serving it with salmon for a colorful, decadent dinner.

4 salmon fillets
¾ teaspoon Himalayan salt, divided
1 tablespoon sesame seeds
2 bunches asparagus (about 24 pieces), woody ends cut off
¼ teaspoon garlic powder
1 tablespoon extra-virgin olive oil
1 tablespoon freshly grated Parmesan cheese
Freshly ground black pepper (optional)

1. Preheat the oven to 400°F. Line 2 baking sheets or dishes with parchment paper (one for asparagus and one for salmon).
2. Place the salmon fillets on a prepared baking sheet and sprinkle with ½ teaspoon of salt and sesame seeds.
3. Bake for 12 to 15 minutes, then remove from the oven and let it rest while you prepare the asparagus.
4. Add asparagus to the other baking sheet, sprinkle with the remaining ¼ teaspoon of salt and garlic powder. Drizzle with the olive oil and toss with hands until well coated.
5. Bake for 10 minutes, until tender.
6. In the last 2 minutes of baking, sprinkle the Parmesan cheese on top.
7. Add black pepper before serving, if desired. Serve the salmon surrounded by asparagus.

❋ **Substitution tip:** You can use vegan Parmesan cheese to make this dish dairy-free.

❋ **Ingredient tip:** Asparagus is best when served immediately after cooking. Storing it in the refrigerator overnight will make it soggy.

Per serving: Calories: 269; Fat: 14g; Protein: 31g; Carbohydrates: 4g; Fiber: 2g; Sodium: 262mg

SEARED SCALLOPS

DAIRY-FREE • GLUTEN-FREE • NUT-FREE • SOY-FREE

Prep time: 15 minutes • **Cook time:** 15 minutes

Yield: 2 servings

Scallops always seemed so fancy to me, especially at restaurants. One day I was flipping through a Gordon Ramsay cookbook and saw a recipe for scallops. I was so surprised to see how very little preparation scallops need! His recipe involved just some salt, black pepper, and butter, and the cooking time was less than 10 minutes. Fast forward to today; I make scallops for special occasions, as they are one of the pricier seafoods to buy, but I'm no longer intimidated by them. Over the years, I've developed a few different scallop recipes and this is one of my favorites. Serve these with Mashed Sweet Potatoes with Spinach (page 107).

8 sea scallops, washed and patted dry
1 tablespoon extra-virgin olive oil plus 1 teaspoon, divided
Juice of ½ lemon
1 clove garlic, crushed
¼ teaspoon Himalayan salt
Freshly ground black pepper (optional)
White truffle oil (optional)

1. In a medium bowl, combine the scallops, 1 tablespoon of olive oil, lemon juice, garlic, and salt. Mix and let marinate for about 15 minutes.
2. Rub the remaining teaspoon of olive oil in a nonstick sauté pan or skillet. Heat the skillet over medium-high heat, and when hot, add the scallops. Sear on one side for about 3 minutes, then flip to the other side for another 2 minutes.
3. Add some freshly ground black pepper and drizzle with white truffle oil, if desired.
4. Serve 4 scallops and some mashed sweet potatoes on each plate and enjoy warm.

* **Prep tip:** The longer you marinate the scallops, the more lemon-garlic flavor they'll have and the faster they will cook. You can even leave the scallops in this marinade overnight in the refrigerator. Before cooking the scallops the next day, it is important to leave them at room temperature for at least 10 to 15 minutes.

Per serving: Calories: 126; Fat: 9g; Protein: 7g; Carbohydrates: 3g; Fiber: 0g; Sodium: 391mg

Chimichurri Sauce
page 159

CHAPTER NINE

DRESSINGS, SAUCES, AND MARINADES

The dressings, sauces, and marinades in this cookbook are so versatile that you will be able to use them with many recipes beyond these. To make them easily accessible to you when you cook, I included them in a separate chapter so that you don't need to flip through the book and hunt for them. Again, I'm all about making clean eating and cooking simple and convenient. I included some tips and suggestions with each of the recipes, as you'll see in coming pages, but feel free to get adventurous and pair these wonderful dressings, sauces, and marinades with anything you see fit.

Basic EVOO and Lemon Dressing **154**

Gochugaru Sesame Seed Dressing with EVOO **155**

Tahini Dressing **156**

Dijon Mustard Dressing **157**

Tangy Mustard Dressing with Apple Cider Vinegar **158**

* Chimichurri Sauce **159**

Mango Salsa **160**

Miso Glaze **161**

Greek Yogurt Marinade **162**

Kefir Marinade **163**

BASIC EVOO AND LEMON DRESSING

DAIRY-FREE • **GLUTEN-FREE** • **NUT-FREE** • **SOY-FREE** • **VEGETARIAN** • **VEGAN**

Prep time: 5 minutes
Yield: About ¼ cup

This simple olive oil and lemon dressing is so versatile, it can be used for many salads, such as Traditional Greek Salad (page 45), Garbanzo Bean Salad (page 46), and simple green salads. I recommend that you use good quality, cold-pressed olive oil—it really makes the difference in taste. Always read the label when buying olive oil, because many brands will say olive oil but add other oils to it.

⅛ cup extra-virgin olive oil
Juice of ½ lemon
½ teaspoon Himalayan salt

Whisk together the olive oil, lemon, and salt. Give a fresh stir right before serving.

✳ **Storage tip:** Store any leftover dressing in a glass container in the refrigerator for up to a few days.

Per serving (2 tablespoons): Calories: 127; Fat: 14g; Protein: 0g; Carbohydrates: 1g; Fiber: 0g; Sodium: 291mg

GOCHUGARU SESAME SEED DRESSING WITH EVOO

DAIRY-FREE · GLUTEN-FREE · NUT-FREE · SOY-FREE · VEGETARIAN

Prep time: 5 minutes

Yield: About ½ cup

This dressing is simple but full of flavor. It pairs wonderfully with simple greens, such as romaine or butter lettuce, but also with cold rice noodles. *Gochugaru* is a special kind of Korean chili flake that is a little less spicy than crushed red pepper flakes. So if you choose to substitute, use a little less. Using toasted sesame seeds will add even more flavor to the dressing. If you wish to use this dressing with rice noodles, replace one part olive oil with sesame oil. This will give you restaurant-style noodles right in your kitchen.

¼ cup extra-virgin olive oil

¼ cup rice vinegar

1 tablespoon sesame seeds

¼ teaspoon gochugaru (Korean chili flakes)

¼ teaspoon Himalayan salt

Whisk together the olive oil, rice vinegar, sesame seeds, gochugaru, and salt. Give a fresh stir right before serving.

✳ **Storage tip:** Store any leftover dressing in a glass container in the refrigerator for up to a few days.

Per serving (2 tablespoons): Calories: 136; Fat: 15g; Protein: 0g; Carbohydrates: 0g; Fiber: 0g; Sodium: 84mg

TAHINI DRESSING

DAIRY-FREE · GLUTEN-FREE · NUT-FREE · SOY-FREE · VEGETARIAN · VEGAN

Prep time: 5 minutes
Yield: About ½ cup

Tahini has become one of the latest health trends because of its dense nutritional profile. Rich in protein, fiber, and good fats, this creamy and nutty paste is made from sesame seeds, which are a great source of calcium, iron, and magnesium. You might know tahini from hummus recipes, but lately tahini has been making appearances in dressings and healthy desserts as well. When combined with other ingredients, tahini becomes more neutral and allows other flavors to come through.

2 tablespoons tahini
2 tablespoons extra-virgin olive oil
Juice of ½ lemon
1 teaspoon honey
1 clove garlic, crushed
¼ teaspoon Himalayan salt

Whisk together the tahini, olive oil, lemon juice, honey, garlic, and salt. Give a fresh stir right before serving.

* **Storage tip:** Store any leftover dressing in a glass container in the refrigerator for up to a three days.

Per serving (2 tablespoons): Calories: 112; Fat: 11g; Protein: 1g; Carbohydrates: 4g; Fiber: 1g; Sodium: 87mg

DIJON MUSTARD DRESSING

DAIRY-FREE • GLUTEN-FREE • NUT-FREE • SOY-FREE • VEGETARIAN • VEGAN

Prep time: 5 minutes

Yield: About ½ cup

Just like spices, dressings are a great way to elevate simple flavors of foods and make them even tastier. This dressing can be used on your favorite salads, but it also tastes great as a dip for Baked Chicken Tenders (page 130). You can also use it as a marinade for grilled meats. While lemon will cure the meat, the Dijon mustard will lock in moisture during cooking. If you want to get creative, try this recipe with whole-grain mustard. The texture of the dressing is wonderful on simple greens such as butter lettuce, or neutral-tasting veggies such as grilled zucchini.

1 teaspoon Dijon mustard
¼ cup extra-virgin olive oil
Juice of 1 large lemon
½ teaspoon Himalayan salt

In a bowl, whisk together the Dijon, olive oil, lemon, and salt. Stir again before serving.

* **Storage tip:** Store any leftover dressing in a glass container in the refrigerator for up to a few days.

Per serving (2 tablespoons): Calories: 123; Fat: 14g; Protein: 0g; Carbohydrates: 1g; Fiber: 0g; Sodium: 160mg

TANGY MUSTARD DRESSING WITH APPLE CIDER VINEGAR

GLUTEN-FREE · NUT-FREE · SOY-FREE · VEGETARIAN

Prep time: 5 minutes

Yield: About ¼ cup

While Dijon Mustard Dressing (page 157) uses lemon and is light in flavor, this mustard dressing uses apple cider vinegar, which makes it richer and tangier—hence its use for heartier dishes, such as cauliflower with quinoa, rather than leafy greens. Of course, technically both dressings can be used on anything at all. You can use this dressing for any type of roasted veggies. I love making a double batch of this dressing and keeping it in the refrigerator to be used with leftover vegetables.

2 tablespoons extra-virgin olive oil

1 tablespoon whole-grain mustard

1 tablespoon Dijon mustard

1 tablespoon apple cider vinegar

In a bowl, whisk together the olive oil, whole-grain mustard, Dijon mustard, and apple cider vinegar. Stir again before serving.

* **Storage tip:** Store any leftover dressing in a glass container in the refrigerator for up to a few days.

Per serving (2 tablespoons): Calories: 130; Fat: 14g; Protein: 1g; Carbohydrates: 1g; Fiber: 1g; Sodium: 173mg

CHIMICHURRI SAUCE

DAIRY-FREE • GLUTEN-FREE • NUT-FREE • SOY-FREE

Prep time: 5 minutes

Yield: About 1 cup

Chimichurri is a popular basting sauce that originated in Argentina and has since been adapted and used all over the world. The original recipe uses olive oil, parsley, garlic, some oregano, and red wine vinegar, but over the years I have experimented with different fresh herbs and it seems you can't go wrong with any combination. Use it over meats and roasted veggies.

½ cup extra-virgin olive oil

2 tablespoons rice vinegar

¼ cup fresh chopped parsley

1 tablespoon fresh chopped basil

1 tablespoon fresh chopped oregano

2 large garlic cloves, minced

¼ teaspoon Himalayan salt

¼ teaspoon freshly ground black pepper

1. In a small bowl, whisk together the olive oil and rice vinegar.
2. Add the parsley, basil, oregano, garlic, salt, and pepper. Mix until well incorporated.
3. Whisk again before using.

✳ **Storage tip:** This makes a double recipe, so any leftover sauce can be stored in a glass container at room temperature for up to 1 week.

Per serving (2 tablespoons): Calories: 122; Fat: 13g; Protein: 0g; Carbohydrates: 0g; Fiber: 0g; Sodium: 40mg

MANGO SALSA

DAIRY-FREE · GLUTEN-FREE · NUT-FREE · SOY-FREE

Prep time: 10 minutes
Yield: About 1 cup

Although it may sound like a new and hip sauce, mango salsa traces its history all the way to the 16th century—to Maya and Incas and their original salsas frescas. This fresh, light salsa pairs beautifully with fish, but it'll also be wonderful served with some baked tortilla chips at your next barbecue!

1 large mango, cut into small cubes
2 tablespoons fresh parsley, chopped
Juice of ½ lemon
1 scallion, chopped (green and white parts)

In a bowl, combine the mango, parsley, lemon juice, and scallion. Mix to blend.

＊ **Storage tip:** Store marinade in a glass container in the refrigerator for up to a few days.

Per serving (¼ cup): Calories: 54; Fat: 0g; Protein: 1g; Carbohydrates: 13g; Fiber: 2g; Sodium: 3mg

MISO GLAZE

DAIRY-FREE • NUT-FREE • VEGETARIAN

Prep time: 3 minutes
Yield: 5 servings

This glaze is wonderful not only for fish, but for shrimp and chicken as well. You can use it as a marinade or as a glaze. Honey in this recipe perfectly balances out the saltiness of the soy sauce, while garlic adds aroma and a perfect aftertaste without being overpowering. When choosing soy sauce, it is preferable to buy organic or ensure that the label states non-GMO. To read more on this topic, see chapter 1, page 13 and chapter 2, page 25.

4 tablespoons soy sauce
2 tablespoons honey
1 tablespoon rice vinegar
1 large garlic clove, minced

In a bowl, whisk together the soy sauce, honey, rice vinegar, and garlic. Whisk again before using.

✳ **Storage tip:** Store glaze in a glass container in the refrigerator for up to a few days.

Per serving (1 tablespoon): Calories: 21; Fat: 0g; Protein: 1g; Carbohydrates: 5g; Fiber: 0g; Sodium: 440mg

GREEK YOGURT MARINADE

GLUTEN-FREE · NUT-FREE · SOY-FREE · VEGETARIAN

Prep time: 5 minutes
Yield: About ¾ cup

If you have ever wondered why poultry is so soft and juicy in restaurants, it's usually because it was marinated in yogurt or kefir, or prepared with sous-vide (cooked for a long time on low heat in a heat-proof plastic bag). The yogurt tenderizes the meat and the lemon cures the meat, so when we cook it, the meat cooks faster and stays tender. Turmeric, cumin, and garlic aid in flavor—but at the same time, they are not overpowering. You can also use this marinade as a dressing over grilled veggies, such as a medley of zucchini, peppers, and onions.

1 (6-ounce) container plain Greek yogurt
½ teaspoon cumin
½ teaspoon turmeric
½ teaspoon garlic powder
½ teaspoon Himalayan salt
Juice from ½ lemon

1. In a large bowl, combine the yogurt with the cumin, turmeric, garlic powder, salt, and lemon juice. Stir to combine.
2. Discard any marinade after using.

✳ **Storage tip:** Store marinade in a glass container in the refrigerator for up to a few days.

Per serving (2 tablespoons): Calories: 22; Fat: 1g; Protein: 1g; Carbohydrates: 2g; Fiber: 0g; Sodium: 111mg

KEFIR MARINADE

GLUTEN-FREE • NUT-FREE • SOY-FREE • VEGETARIAN

Prep time: 5 minutes
Yield: About 1 cup

Just like yogurt, kefir marinade will help chicken cook faster. Kefir is fermented milk made with "starter" kefir culture—that is, culture grains. It's considered a probiotic because it's full of gut-friendly bacteria. Although it contains lactose, it is digested differently in our gut from regular milk; this is why some people who have mild lactose intolerance can actually digest kefir better than they can milk. You may use regular yogurt or Greek yogurt in this recipe as well; it won't impact the taste. Feel free to use different spices and fresh herbs to change the flavor.

1 cup kefir
Juice of ½ lemon
3 garlic cloves, minced
1 teaspoon oregano
½ to 1 teaspoon Himalayan salt

1. In a large bowl, combine the kefir, lemon juice, garlic, oregano, and salt. Mix together well.
2. Discard any marinade after using.

✳ **Substitution tip:** You can use yogurt instead of kefir. You can also use unsweetened, plain cashew yogurt if you wish to make the marinade dairy-free.

Per serving (2 tablespoons): Calories: 17; Fat: 0g; Protein: 1g; Carbohydrates: 3g; Fiber: 0g; Sodium: 85mg

Tumeric Ginger Latte
page 170

CHAPTER TEN

BEVERAGES AND DESSERTS

All food fits. Period. We can enjoy all the foods we please, truly, but all in moderation. Life Is too short to miss out on traditional crêpes in France, baklava in Turkey, full-fat creamy gelato in Rome, and delicious Levain Bakery chocolate chip cookies in New York City. Having said that, it is not about what we do *sometimes* that will shape our lives. It is what we do most of the time. It's about our daily choices. I hope you find your favorite new desserts in this chapter. All of them are simple to make, plus they are nutrient-dense and delicious. Enjoy.

Peanut Butter and Banana Smoothie 166

Green Smoothie 167

Strawberry-Peach Smoothie 168

Coconut-Pineapple Smoothie 169

* Turmeric Ginger Latte 170

Homemade Chocolate Spread 171

Strawberry Chia Jam 172

Buckwheat Crêpes 173

Chocolate Peanut Butter Truffles 174

Protein Rice Crisps 175

Banana Nice-Cream 176

Strawberry Ice Pops 177

PEANUT BUTTER AND BANANA SMOOTHIE

DAIRY-FREE • GLUTEN-FREE • NUT-FREE • SOY-FREE • VEGAN

Prep time: 5 minutes
Yield: 2 servings

Smoothies can make a great breakfast or snack—if they are made well. That is, if they are nutritionally balanced. A well-balanced smoothie should contain protein, fiber, and some healthy fats. In this case, both peanut butter and almond milk provide plant-based protein, fiber, and good fats; banana adds the sweetness via natural sugars; and vanilla protein powder adds additional protein. The spinach adds vitamins and iron, but you don't even taste it.

12 ounces vanilla almond milk
1 banana, frozen
1 measure plant-based, vanilla protein powder
1 tablespoon peanut butter
1 cup baby spinach

1. In a high-speed blender, combine the milk, banana, protein powder, peanut butter, and spinach.
2. Blend until creamy and enjoy.

* **Substitution tips:** Vanilla whey protein works wonderfully as well. Kale may be used instead of spinach. If allergic to peanuts, you can use almond butter. Finally, you can omit the protein powder and use egg whites instead. I heard about this trick from a friend of mine. She used egg whites often instead of whey protein powder as her protein source. Instead of protein powder, add about ¼ cup egg whites to 6 ounces of milk. Blend and enjoy!

Per serving: Calories: 256; Fat: 8g; Protein: 16g; Carbohydrates: 34g; Fiber: 5g; Sodium: 123mg

GREEN SMOOTHIE

DAIRY-FREE · GLUTEN-FREE · NUT-FREE · SOY-FREE · VEGAN

Prep time: 5 minutes
Yield: 1 serving

This light and cleansing smoothie is so refreshing and feels good any time of year. The veggies in this smoothie are neutral and apple adds the perfect sweetness, while the avocado makes this green smoothie super creamy and extra delicious!

2 cups baby spinach
¼ avocado
½ cucumber
½ lemon, squeezed
½ apple
1 cup water

1. In a high-speed blender, combine the spinach, avocado, cucumber, lemon, apple, and water.
2. Blend until smooth.
3. Enjoy right away or refrigerate for up to several hours.

✳ **Substitution tip:** You can use pear instead of apple, and lime instead of lemon.

Per serving: Calories: 180; Fat: 8g; Protein: 5g; Carbohydrates: 28g; Fiber: 9g; Sodium: 53mg

STRAWBERRY-PEACH SMOOTHIE

DAIRY-FREE • GLUTEN-FREE • NUT-FREE • SOY-FREE • VEGAN

Prep time: 5 minutes
Yield: 1 serving

When berries and peaches are in season, this is one of my favorite breakfast smoothies to make. Almond milk and oat bran add extra protein and fiber, while the honey adds the perfect touch of sweetness. This smoothie is refreshing, filling, and a great source of antioxidants.

10 large strawberries, hulled
½ peach, frozen
1 cup unsweetened almond milk
2 tablespoons oat bran
1 tablespoon raw honey

1. In a high-speed blender, combine the strawberries, peach, almond milk, oat bran, and honey.
2. Blend to desired consistency.
3. Drink right away or refrigerate for up to several hours.

* **Substitution tip:** You can use frozen strawberries if strawberries are not in season. You may just need to add a little extra almond milk to make this beverage less like ice cream and more like a smoothie.

Per serving: Calories: 271; Fat: 4g; Protein: 5g; Carbohydrates: 62g; Fiber: 8g; Sodium: 154mg

COCONUT-PINEAPPLE SMOOTHIE

DAIRY-FREE • GLUTEN-FREE • NUT-FREE • SOY-FREE • VEGAN

Prep time: 5 minutes

Yield: 1 serving

Did you notice that I added some greens to almost every smoothie in this cookbook? That's because greens like iceberg and spinach are so neutral that you won't even notice them in the smoothie, but you will enjoy the benefits of their nutrition. This smoothie combines coconut and pineapple, which are both really flavorful and good for our digestive systems. I make this smoothie anytime I need extra cleansing and "debloating." Coconut is known for its anti-inflammatory properties, while the bromelain in pineapple aids in protein absorption and digestion.

1 cup fresh pineapple

¼ cup shredded, unsweetened coconut

1 cup iceberg lettuce

1 cup water

1. In a high-speed blender, combine the pineapple, coconut, lettuce, and water.
2. Blend until smooth.
3. Drink right away or refrigerate for up to several hours.

∗ **Substitution tip:** You can use frozen pineapple instead of fresh. If you buy canned pineapple, check to make sure there is no added sugar. If you like extra coconut flavor, add unsweetened coconut water instead of plain water.

∗ **Prep tip:** For an ice-cream-like smoothie, you can add frozen pineapple and reduce the water by a little bit. You can even add this smoothie to an ice pop mold and freeze it overnight for a delicious summertime refresher.

Per serving: Calories: 163; Fat: 7g; Protein: 2g; Carbohydrates: 27g; Fiber: 5g; Sodium: 13mg

TURMERIC GINGER LATTE

DAIRY-FREE · GLUTEN-FREE · NUT-FREE · SOY-FREE · VEGAN

Prep time: 5 minutes

Yield: 2 servings

Two of the strongest antioxidants are ginger and turmeric. To get familiar with the flavors of turmeric and ginger, I suggest starting with simple teas. Make pure ginger and pure turmeric tea daily and let your body get accustomed to the taste. It does take time to get used to these two spices because they are very strong in taste. This turmeric ginger latte is on the spicy side, but the vanilla and honey really balance it out. Once you make the recipe once, you can always adjust the amount of each ingredient to your liking.

12 ounces unsweetened vanilla almond milk

1 teaspoon turmeric

½ teaspoon ground ginger

¼ teaspoon cinnamon

1 teaspoon raw honey

1. In a small saucepan, bring the vanilla almond milk to a boil.
2. Remove from heat and add the turmeric, ginger, cinnamon, and honey. Whisk well until combined.
3. Drink warm.

* **Ingredient tip:** When selecting ginger and turmeric, opt for organic and bioavailable kinds, as opposed to the ones you get as a spice at the grocery store. Your body can much more easily absorb the bioavailable spices than store-bought spices.

* **Substitution tip:** You can use unsweetened almond milk or oat milk as well, but in that case, add ¼ teaspoon of vanilla extract.

Per serving: Calories: 75; Fat: 2g; Protein: 1g; Carbohydrates: 13g; Fiber: 2g; Sodium: 108mg

HOMEMADE CHOCOLATE SPREAD

DAIRY-FREE • GLUTEN-FREE • NUT-FREE • SOY-FREE • VEGAN

Prep time: 5 minutes
Yield: 2 cups

I won't say that this spread tastes like store-bought chocolate hazelnut spread, but I will tell you that it's just as delicious and much more nutritious. And yes, guilt-free! I do not like to say "guilt-free food" because all food should be enjoyed and no food should make us feel guilty. We make choices and some days we choose less healthy foods and that is okay. But what's important is that on most days we choose healthier and more nutritious alternatives such as this one. This chocolate spread is high in fiber and protein and full of good fats coming from the tahini and flax seeds. There is no refined sugar in this recipe either—the sweetness comes from banana and honey.

1 cup tahini
1 large banana, mashed
½ cup raw cacao
3 tablespoons oat groats
3 tablespoons ground flaxseed
¼ cup raw honey
¼ cup coconut oil, melted

1. In a high-speed blender or food processor, combine the tahini, banana, cacao, oat groats, flaxseed, honey, and coconut oil.
2. Pulse to desired consistency, but avoid over-blending.
3. Store in a glass container at room temperature for up to 3 days. If storing longer, transfer to the refrigerator.

* **Serving tip:** This spread is wonderful on whole-grain toast, high-fiber crackers, or rice cakes.

* **Substitution tips:** You can replace oat groats with oat bran.

Per serving (1 tablespoon): Calories: 81; Fat: 6g; Protein: 2g; Carbohydrates: 6g; Fiber: 2g; Sodium: 9mg

STRAWBERRY CHIA JAM

DAIRY-FREE • GLUTEN-FREE • NUT-FREE • SOY-FREE • VEGAN

Prep time: 5 minutes • **Cook time:** 25 minutes
Yield: About ¾ cup

The smell of freshly cooked jam takes me straight back to my childhood. Every summer we went strawberry and raspberry picking up in the mountains, and then our parents would make jam and juice. At the time, white sugar was commonly used and there was no chia. Despite the white sugar, I think that jam was much healthier than most jams you can buy today at the stores. Today, companies use artificial colors and flavors and add additives to jams for a longer shelf life. When buying jams, consider getting some from your local farm and make sure to read the label.

2 cups frozen strawberries
3 tablespoons coconut sugar
1 cup water
2 tablespoons vanilla extract
2 tablespoons chia seeds

1. In a medium stockpot, combine the strawberries, coconut sugar, water, and vanilla, and bring to boil.
2. Cover and cook for 15 to 20 minutes, until the strawberries have cooked down and the mixture has thickened.
3. Add the chia seeds and cook for 3 more minutes.
4. Let the jam cool before transferring it to a glass jar for storage.

* **Substitution tip:** You can use frozen raspberries or any frozen berry mixture. You may need to adjust the sweetness depending on the kind of berries you use.

Per serving (1 tablespoon): Calories: 37; Fat: 0g; Protein: 0g; Carbohydrates: 7g; Fiber: 1g; Sodium: 1mg

BUCKWHEAT CRÊPES

DAIRY-FREE · GLUTEN-FREE · NUT-FREE · SOY-FREE · VEGETARIAN

Prep time: 5 minutes · **Cook time:** 20 minutes
Yield: 6 crepes

Crêpes are traditionally made with white flour, milk, and eggs. Favorite toppings around the world include jam, chocolate hazelnut spread, or sugar with lime. While we make standard crepes often, I also like to modify the original recipe and make them a little more nutrient-dense. One way of doing this is replacing white flour with high-protein flours such as spelt or einkorn, or adding almond milk instead of regular milk. This recipe uses buckwheat flour, which gives crêpes a great nutty flavor. And sparkling water makes these crepes extra fluffy!

1 large egg, beaten
¼ cup buckwheat flour
¼ cup rice flour
¾ cup sparkling water
1 teaspoon vanilla extract
Coconut oil for greasing the crêpe pan

1. In a medium bowl, combine the egg and buckwheat and rice flours. Stir until incorporated.
2. Add the sparkling water, mix, and see how thick the batter is. It should be a little thinner than pancake batter.
3. Add the vanilla and stir.
4. In a nonstick pan, melt the coconut oil and bake crêpes as usual.
5. Add your favorite spread inside, along with some berries on top.

* **Serving tip:** For the toppings, I recommend the Homemade Chocolate Spread (page 171) or Strawberry Chia Jam (page 172). Fresh berries are always nice on top.

* **Substitution tip:** You can use just buckwheat flour instead of mixing it with rice flour.

Per serving (2 crêpes): Calories: 116; Fat: 3g; Protein: 4g; Carbohydrates: 18g; Fiber: 1g; Sodium: 25mg

CHOCOLATE PEANUT BUTTER TRUFFLES

DAIRY-FREE · GLUTEN-FREE · SOY-FREE · VEGAN
Prep time: 5 minutes, plus overnight to freeze
Yield: 12 truffles

Dates make a great sugar substitute. Although they have a particular taste, when you add dates to desserts, they sweeten without really changing the flavor profile. Somehow, they become neutral when combined with other ingredients, and especially when combined with nuts and seeds. The glycemic index of dates is lower than sugar, so it impacts our blood sugar to a lesser extent. Dates contain some protein and fiber, as well as iron, magnesium, vitamin B_6, and calcium. Enjoy them along with dark chocolate and walnuts in this yummy sweet treat.

1 cup walnuts
12 fresh dates, pitted
1 cup tahini
½ cup chocolate peanut butter powder
3½ ounces dark chocolate (at least 85 percent dark)

1. Soak the walnuts and dates for at least 30 minutes (see Prep tip).
2. Combine the walnuts and dates in a blender or food processor and blend until the mixture is thick and sticky. Transfer to a bowl.
3. Add the tahini and chocolate peanut butter powder and mix until well incorporated.
4. Form the batter into 12 bite-size balls, put them on a plate, and freeze for 15 minutes.
5. Melt most of the chocolate and spoon some over the semi-frozen truffles. Shred the rest of the chocolate for topping.
6. Sprinkle with some shredded chocolate. Put the truffles back in the freezer overnight.
7. The next day, transfer the truffles to a covered glass container and refrigerate for up to a few days.

* **Prep tip:** When you finish soaking the walnuts and dates, save a quarter of the soaking liquid in case the mixture is too thick and can't blend.

* **Substitution tip:** The chocolate peanut butter powder can be replaced by ¼ cup raw cacao and 2 tablespoons creamy peanut butter.

* **Ingredient tip:** When buying pitted dates, pay attention to the ingredient label to make sure no sugar is added. It's even better if you buy fresh dates and then pit them yourself.

Per serving (1 truffle): Calories: 180; Fat: 14g; Protein: 5g; Carbohydrates: 10g; Fiber: 3g; Sodium: 42mg

PROTEIN RICE CRISPS

DAIRY-FREE • GLUTEN-FREE • NUT-FREE • SOY-FREE • VEGAN
Prep time: 5 minutes, plus 20 minutes to freeze
Yield: 6 to 8 crisps

This is what I call "adult Rice Krispies treats." The traditional variety is pure sugar (or should I say syrup?) with artificial ingredients in between. These clean treats are made with puffed rice, pumpkin seeds, and plant-based protein. Dark chocolate with maple binds it all together for a perfect bite. Even kids love them! I used maple syrup in this recipe, but feel free to use raw honey instead—just add ½ teaspoon vanilla extract to replace the touch of maple. If you are making these for kids, omit the protein powder.

7 ounces dark chocolate (at least 85 percent), melted
3 tablespoons maple syrup
1 teaspoon coconut oil (optional)
2 cups puffed rice
2 tablespoons plant-based vanilla protein powder
4 tablespoons pumpkin seeds

1. In a heat-proof bowl, combine the chocolate, maple syrup, and coconut oil (if using), and melt it in the microwave in 30-second increments, stirring in between. Set aside.
2. In a medium bowl, combine the puffed rice, vanilla protein powder, and pumpkin seeds. Mix together.
3. Pour the chocolate mixture over the rice mixture and stir to combine.
4. Line an 8-by-8-inch baking dish with parchment paper and spread the rice crispy mixture to about 1 finger thickness.
5. Freeze for about 20 minutes. Break the treats into small pieces and store covered in the refrigerator.

✳ **Substitution tips:** You can use any kind of seeds or nuts instead of pumpkin seeds; just chop them small. Also, dark chocolate may be replaced with dark chocolate chips.

Per serving: Calories: 225; Fat: 13g; Protein: 6g; Carbohydrates: 22g; Fiber: 3g; Sodium: 48mg

BANANA NICE-CREAM

DAIRY-FREE • GLUTEN-FREE • NUT-FREE • SOY-FREE • VEGAN

Prep time: 5 minutes
Yield: 2 servings

There is a time and place for everything. You are on the beach enjoying the weather and choose an ice pop to cool you down. The next time, you're walking around Venice, you spot the cutest gelato place. You stop and have 2 scoops of your favorite salted caramel and pistachio. Now you are at home, craving something cold and sweet. There is ice cream in the freezer, but there are also some frozen bananas. Then you opt to make this nice-cream!

3½ large bananas, cut in half, frozen
¼ cup vanilla almond milk
1 tablespoon maple syrup
½ fresh banana, for topping
1 tablespoon cacao nibs

1. In a high-speed blender, combine the frozen bananas, almond milk, and maple syrup.
2. Start blending on a low speed. As the bananas break down, increase the speed.
3. Blend until you get a thick ice-cream-like consistency.
4. Scoop the nice-cream into a serving bowl and add some fresh bananas and cacao nibs on top.
5. Enjoy immediately.

* **Substitution tips:** You can use any plant-based milk of your choice. Chocolate chips may be used instead of cacao nibs for the topping.

Per serving: Calories: 302; Fat: 4g; Protein: 4g; Carbohydrates: 72g; Fiber: 8g; Sodium: 23mg

STRAWBERRY ICE POPS

DAIRY-FREE · GLUTEN-FREE · NUT-FREE · SOY-FREE · VEGAN

Prep time: 5 minutes, plus overnight to freeze
Yield: 4 to 6 pops

This is a basic ice pop recipe that you will keep making over and over again. The best part is you can replace the ingredients as you see fit. Any kind of berries can replace strawberries, maple syrup can replace honey, and you can use lemon, water, or coconut water instead of orange juice. So many combinations, and they're all truly delicious!

2 cups fresh strawberries
2 tablespoons raw honey
½ cup orange juice

1. In a high-speed blender, combine the strawberries, honey, and orange juice.
2. Blend to desired consistency.
3. Fill up the ice pop molds and freeze overnight.

＊ **Ingredient tip:** While these are great for kids and kids at heart, children younger than 1 year old should not eat honey—it contains bacteria that can be harmful to them.

＊ **Seasonal tip:** When strawberries are not in season, you can use frozen strawberries.

＊ **Prep tip:** When buying orange juice, select the "no sugar added" kind.

Per serving: Calories: 70; Fat: 0g; Protein: 1g; Carbohydrates: 18g; Fiber: 2g; Sodium: 2mg

INDEX

A

Adzuki Bean Soup, 90
American Protein Pancakes, 31
Apples
    Green Smoothie, 167
    Oatmeal with Baked Apples and
        Walnuts, 20
Arugula
    Arugula Salad with Baked Acorn Squash and
        Pomegranate Seeds, 53
    Arugula Watermelon Salad, 48
    Green Lentil Salad with Dijon Mustard
        Dressing, 93
Asparagus
    Baked Salmon with Parmesan
        Asparagus, 149
    Lemony Asparagus Risotto, 78
Avocados, 5
    Arugula Watermelon Salad, 48
    Avocado Corn Salad with Tahini Dressing, 51
    Buddha Bowl, 110
    Classic Guacamole, 59
    Collard Green Wraps with Vegetables and
        Tahini Dressing, 101
    Green Smoothie, 167
    Quinoa Burrito Bowl, 109

B

Baked Beans in Tomato Sauce, 88
Baked Chicken Tenders, 130
Baked Chicken Wings with Sriracha Glaze, 65
Baked Cod Fillets in Mushroom Sauce, 141
Baked Salmon with Parmesan Asparagus, 149
Baked Sunny-Side Up Eggs with Zoodles, 29
Baked Sweet Potato Fries with Spicy Yogurt
        Sauce, 62–63
Baked Tuna Melts, 61
Bananas
    Banana Nice-Cream, 176
    Homemade Chocolate Spread, 171
    Peanut Butter and Banana Smoothie, 166

Basic EVOO and Lemon Dressing, 154
Basil
    Chimichurri Sauce, 159
    Eggplant Parm, 112
    Shrimp Saganaki, 144–145
Beans
    Adzuki Bean Soup, 90
    Baked Beans in Tomato Sauce, 88
    Beans with Baby Spinach, 89
    Beet and Bean Hummus, 71
    Buddha Bowl, 110
    Cold Bean Salad, 49
    Kale and Bean Soup with Tofu, 102
    String Bean Casserole with Chicken, 87
Beef
    Beef Burgers Stuffed with Feta and
        Prosciutto, 135
    Grass-Fed Sirloin Steak with Chimichurri, 134
Beets, 5
    Beet and Bean Hummus, 71
    Roasted Beet Salad, 47
Berries, 5
    Honey-Almond Greek Yogurt with
        Berries, 57
    Overnight Chia Pudding with Berries, 24
    Strawberry Chia Jam, 172
    Strawberry Ice Pops, 177
    Strawberry-Peach Smoothie, 168
Beverages. *See also* Smoothies
    Turmeric Ginger Latte, 170
Bowls
    Buddha Bowl, 110
    Quinoa Burrito Bowl, 109
BPA (bisphenol A), 13
Braised Cabbage with Chicken, 131
Branzino, Roasted, with Lemon Potatoes, 147
Broccoli, 5
    Broccoli Pizza Crust, 67
    Creamy Broccoli Soup, 37–38
    Creamy Chicken and Broccoli Pasta, 96–97
    Veggie Minestrone Soup, 39

Brussels sprouts
    Arugula Salad with Baked Acorn Squash and
        Pomegranate Seeds, 53
Buckwheat Crêpes, 173
Buddha Bowl, 110
Burgers
    Beef Burgers Stuffed with Feta and
        Prosciutto, 135
    Mexican-Inspired Turkey Burgers, 126
    Tuna Burgers, 139
Butter Lettuce with Sesame Dressing, 44

C

Cabbage, 5. *See also* Coleslaw
    Braised Cabbage with Chicken, 131
Canned goods, 9–10
Capers, Lemon Chicken with, 128
Carrots
    Adzuki Bean Soup, 90
    Braised Cabbage with Chicken, 131
    Creamy Broccoli Soup, 37–38
    Green Lentil Stew, 91
    Pea Stew with Chicken, 85–86
    Raw Veggies with Yogurt Tzatziki, 58
    String Bean Casserole with Chicken, 87
    Swiss Chard Rolls with Rice in Tomato
        Sauce, 81–82
    Tuna Lettuce Cups, 60
    Tuna Salad, 140
    Veal Goulash, 133
    Veggie Cauliflower Rice, 106
Cauliflower
    Cauliflower Chickpea Stew with Turmeric, 113
    Creamy Broccoli Soup, 37–38
    Chickpea Pasta with Mushrooms and
        Sage, 117–118
    Roasted Cauliflower with Quinoa and
        Mustard Dressing, 105
    Tandoori Cauliflower Curry, 114
    Veggie Cauliflower Rice, 106
Celery, 5
    Adzuki Bean Soup, 90
    Green Lentil Stew, 91
    Spicy Tomato Bisque, 41–42
    Swiss Chard Zucchini Soup, 40
Cheese. *See also* Cream cheese
    Arugula Watermelon Salad, 48

Baked Salmon with Parmesan
    Asparagus, 149
Baked Tuna Melts, 61
Beef Burgers Stuffed with Feta and
    Prosciutto, 135
Creamy Broccoli Soup, 37–38
Eggplant Parm, 112
Lemony Asparagus Risotto, 78
Omelet with Spinach and Goat Cheese, 26
Roasted Beet Salad, 47
Savory Corn Muffins with Spinach and
    Feta, 33
Shakshuka, 27–28
Shrimp Saganaki, 144–145
Shrimp with Zoodles, 143
Stuffed Mushrooms with Spinach and Goat
    Cheese, 66
Vegan Lasagna, 119
Chia seeds, 5, 7
    Overnight Chia Pudding with Berries, 24
    Overnight Chia and Quinoa Pudding with
        Coconut, 22
    Strawberry Chia Jam, 172
    Yogurt Chia Pudding, 23
Chicken
    Baked Chicken Tenders, 130
    Baked Chicken Wings with Sriracha Glaze, 65
    Braised Cabbage with Chicken, 131
    Creamy Chicken and Broccoli Pasta, 96–97
    Greek-Style Grilled Chicken, 129
    Lemon Chicken with Capers, 128
    Pea Stew with Chicken, 85–86
    String Bean Casserole with Chicken, 87
Chickpeas
    Cauliflower Chickpea Stew with Turmeric, 113
    Garbanzo Bean Salad, 46
    Veggie Minestrone Soup, 39
Chimichurri Sauce, 159
Chives
    Baked Sunny-Side Up Eggs with Zoodles, 29
    Cucumber Slices with Vegan Cream Cheese
        and Chives, 72
    Tuna Lettuce Cups, 60
Chocolate
    Banana Nice-Cream, 176
    Chocolate Peanut Butter Truffles, 174
    Homemade Chocolate Spread, 171

Chocolate (*continued*)
    Overnight Chia Pudding with Berries, 24
    Protein Rice Crisps, 175
Cilantro
    Classic Guacamole, 59
Classic Cinnamon Oatmeal, 19
Classic Guacamole, 59
Clean eating, about, 2–4
Clean Fifteen list, 12–13
Coconut, 5
    Coconut Oat Bran, 21
    Coconut-Pineapple Smoothie, 169
    Homemade Granola, 18
    Overnight Chia and Quinoa Pudding with
        Coconut, 22
Cod
    Baked Cod Fillets in Mushroom
        Sauce, 141
    Codfish Risotto with Saffron, 142
Cold Bean Salad, 49
Cold Pasta Salad, 116
Coleslaw
    Vegan Tacos, 111
Collard Green Wraps with Vegetables and
    Tahini Dressing, 101
Cream cheese
    Creamy Chicken and Broccoli Pasta,
        96–97
    Cucumber Slices with Vegan Cream Cheese
        and Chives, 72
    Chickpea Pasta with Mushrooms and
        Sage, 117–118
Creamy Broccoli Soup, 37–38
Creamy Chicken and Broccoli Pasta, 96–97
Crispy Baked Tofu, 103
Cucumbers
    Buddha Bowl, 110
    Butter Lettuce with Sesame Dressing, 44
    Cold Pasta Salad, 116
    Collard Green Wraps with Vegetables and
        Tahini Dressing, 101
    Cucumber Slices with Vegan Cream Cheese
        and Chives, 72
    Garbanzo Bean Salad, 46
    Greek-Style Quinoa Salad, 77
    Green Smoothie, 167
    Quinoa Tabbouleh, 108

    Raw Veggies with Yogurt Tzatziki, 58
    Traditional Greek Salad, 45

D
Dairy-free
    American Protein Pancakes, 31
    Baked Chicken Tenders, 130
    Baked Chicken Wings with Sriracha Glaze, 65
    Baked Cod Fillets in Mushroom Sauce, 141
    Baked Sunny-Side Up Eggs with Zoodles, 29
    Baked Tuna Melts, 61
    Banana Nice-Cream, 176
    Basic EVOO and Lemon Dressing, 154
    Broccoli Pizza Crust, 67
    Buckwheat Crêpes, 173
    Buddha Bowl, 110
    Butter Lettuce with Sesame Dressing, 44
    Cauliflower Chickpea Stew with Turmeric, 113
    Chimichurri Sauce, 159
    Chocolate Peanut Butter Truffles, 174
    Classic Cinnamon Oatmeal, 19
    Classic Guacamole, 59
    Coconut Oat Bran, 21
    Coconut-Pineapple Smoothie, 169
    Codfish Risotto with Saffron, 142
    Cold Pasta Salad, 116
    Collard Green Wraps with Vegetables and
        Tahini Dressing, 101
    Crispy Baked Tofu, 103
    Dijon Mustard Dressing, 157
    Eggplant Parm, 112
    Garbanzo Bean Salad, 46
    Gluten-Free Veggie Ramen Noodle Soup, 43
    Gochugaru Sesame Seed Dressing with
        EVOO, 155
    Grass-Fed Sirloin Steak with Chimichurri, 134
    Green Smoothie, 167
    Grilled Ahi Tuna, 138
    Homemade Chocolate Spread, 171
    Homemade Granola, 18
    Kale and Bean Soup with Tofu, 102
    Kale Salad with Roasted Butternut
        Squash, 52
    Lemon Chicken with Capers, 128
    Chickpea Pasta with Mushrooms and
        Sage, 117–118
    Mango Salsa, 160

Mashed Sweet Potatoes with Spinach, 107
Mexican-Inspired Turkey Burgers, 126
Miso Glaze, 161
Miso-Glazed Salmon, 148
Oatmeal with Baked Apples and Walnuts, 20
Overnight Chia and Quinoa Pudding with
    Coconut, 22
Peanut Butter and Banana Smoothie, 166
Pea Stew with Chicken, 85–86
Protein Rice Crisps, 175
Protein Waffles with Spinach, 32
Quinoa Burrito Bowl, 109
Quinoa Tabbouleh, 108
Roasted Branzino with Lemon Potatoes, 147
Roasted Cauliflower with Quinoa and
    Mustard Dressing, 105
Rosemary Zucchini Tomato Bake, 115
Scrambled Tofu, 25
Seared Scallops, 150
Shrimp Tacos with Mango Salsa, 146
Spaghetti Squash with Vegan
    Bolognese, 120–121
Spicy Shrimp Pasta Arrabbiata, 94–95
Spicy Tomato Bisque, 41–42
Strawberry Chia Jam, 172
Strawberry Ice Pops, 177
Strawberry-Peach Smoothie, 168
Swiss Chard Zucchini Soup, 40
Tahini Dressing, 156
Tandoori Cauliflower Curry, 114
Teriyaki Tofu, 104
Tuna Burgers, 139
Tuna Lettuce Cups, 60
Tuna Salad, 140
Turkey Bolognese, 125
Turmeric Ginger Latte, 170
Unstuffed Stuffed Peppers, 127
Veal Goulash, 133
Vegan Lasagna, 119
Vegan Tacos, 111
Veggie Cauliflower Rice, 106
Veggie Egg Muffins, 30
Veggie Minestrone Soup, 39
Dates
    Chocolate Peanut Butter Truffles, 174
    Overnight Chia and Quinoa Pudding with
        Coconut, 22

Desserts
    Banana Nice-Cream, 176
    Chocolate Peanut Butter Truffles, 174
    Protein Rice Crisps, 175
Dijon Mustard Dressing, 157
Dill
    Raw Veggies with Yogurt Tzatziki, 58
Dips and spreads
    Beet and Bean Hummus, 71
    Classic Guacamole, 59
    Homemade Chocolate Spread, 171
    Mango Salsa, 160
    Raw Veggies with Yogurt Tzatziki, 58
    Roasted Eggplant Dip, 73
    Strawberry Chia Jam, 172
Dirty Dozen list, 12–13
Dressings
    Basic EVOO and Lemon Dressing, 154
    Dijon Mustard Dressing, 157
    Gochugaru Sesame Seed Dressing with
        EVOO, 155
    Tahini Dressing, 156
    Tangy Mustard Dressing with Apple Cider
        Vinegar, 158
Dry goods, 10

E
Eggplants
    Eggplant Parm, 112
    Roasted Eggplant Dip, 73
Eggs
    American Protein Pancakes, 31
    Baked Chicken Tenders, 130
    Baked Sunny-Side Up Eggs with Zoodles, 29
    Broccoli Pizza Crust, 67
    Buckwheat Crêpes, 173
    Mexican-Inspired Turkey Burgers, 126
    Omelet with Spinach and Goat Cheese, 26
    Protein Waffles with Spinach, 32
    Savory Corn Muffins with Spinach and
        Feta, 33
    Shakshuka, 27–28
    String Bean Casserole with Chicken, 87
    Tri-Colored Pepper Medley with Brown
        Rice, 83–84
    Veggie Egg Muffins, 30
Environmental Working Group (EWG), 12–13

F

Fish
   Baked Cod Fillets in Mushroom Sauce, 141
   Baked Salmon with Parmesan
      Asparagus, 149
   Baked Tuna Melts, 61
   Codfish Risotto with Saffron, 142
   Grilled Ahi Tuna, 138
   Miso-Glazed Salmon, 148
   Roasted Branzino with Lemon Potatoes, 147
   Salmon, 6
   Tuna Burgers, 139
   Tuna Lettuce Cups, 60
   Tuna Salad, 140
Flaxseed, 6, 7
   Classic Cinnamon Oatmeal, 19
   Coconut Oat Bran, 21
   Flaxseed Sesame Protein Crackers, 68
   Gluten-Free Biscuits with Pumpkin and
      Sunflower Seeds, 69–70
   Homemade Chocolate Spread, 171
Freezer staples, 11
Fruits, 4, 11–13. *See also specific*

G

Garbanzo Bean Salad, 46
Ginger, 6
Gluten-free
   Adzuki Bean Soup, 90
   American Protein Pancakes, 31
   Arugula Salad with Baked Acorn Squash and
      Pomegranate Seeds, 53
   Arugula Watermelon Salad, 48
   Avocado Corn Salad with Tahini Dressing, 51
   Baked Beans in Tomato Sauce, 88
   Baked Chicken Tenders, 130
   Baked Chicken Wings with
      Sriracha Glaze, 65
   Baked Cod Fillets in Mushroom Sauce, 141
   Baked Salmon with Parmesan
      Asparagus, 149
   Baked Sunny-Side Up Eggs with Zoodles, 29
   Baked Sweet Potato Fries with Spicy Yogurt
      Sauce, 62–63
   Banana Nice-Cream, 176
   Basic EVOO and Lemon Dressing, 154
   Beans with Baby Spinach, 89

Beef Burgers Stuffed with Feta and
   Prosciutto, 135
Beet and Bean Hummus, 71
Braised Cabbage with Chicken, 131
Broccoli Pizza Crust, 67
Buckwheat Crêpes, 173
Buddha Bowl, 110
Butter Lettuce with Sesame Dressing, 44
Cauliflower Chickpea Stew with
   Turmeric, 113
Chickpea Pasta with Mushrooms and
   Sage, 117–118
Chimichurri Sauce, 159
Chocolate Peanut Butter Truffles, 174
Classic Cinnamon Oatmeal, 19
Classic Guacamole, 59
Coconut Oat Bran, 21
Coconut-Pineapple Smoothie, 169
Codfish Risotto with Saffron, 142
Cold Bean Salad, 49
Cold Pasta Salad, 116
Collard Green Wraps with Vegetables and
   Tahini Dressing, 101
Creamy Broccoli Soup, 37–38
Crispy Baked Tofu, 103
Cucumber Slices with Vegan Cream Cheese
   and Chives, 72
Dijon Mustard Dressing, 157
Eggplant Parm, 112
Flaxseed Sesame Protein Crackers, 68
Garbanzo Bean Salad, 46
Gluten-Free Biscuits with Pumpkin and
   Sunflower Seeds, 69–70
Gluten-Free Veggie Ramen Noodle Soup, 43
Gochugaru Sesame Seed Dressing with
   EVOO, 155
Grass-Fed Sirloin Steak with Chimichurri, 134
Greek–Style Grilled Chicken, 129
Greek–Style Quinoa Salad, 77
Greek Yogurt Marinade, 162
Green Lentil Salad with Dijon Mustard
   Dressing, 93
Green Lentil Stew, 91
Green Smoothie, 167
Grilled Ahi Tuna, 138
Grilled Turkey Breast Marinated in
   Yogurt, 124

Homemade Chocolate Spread, 171
Homemade Granola, 18
Honey-Almond Greek Yogurt with Berries, 57
Kale and Bean Soup with Tofu, 102
Kale Salad with Roasted Butternut Squash, 52
Kefir Marinade, 163
Lemon Chicken with Capers, 128
Lemony Asparagus Risotto, 78
Lentil Bisque, 92
Chickpea Pasta with Mushrooms and
    Sage, 117–118
Mango Salsa, 160
Mashed Sweet Potatoes with Spinach, 107
Mexican–Inspired Turkey Burgers, 126
Oatmeal with Baked Apples and Walnuts, 20
Omelet with Spinach and Goat Cheese, 26
Overnight Chia and Quinoa Pudding with
    Coconut, 22
Overnight Chia Pudding with Berries, 24
Peanut Butter and Banana Smoothie, 166
Pea Stew with Chicken, 85–86
Protein Rice Crisps, 175
Protein Waffles with Spinach, 32
Quinoa Burrito Bowl, 109
Quinoa Tabbouleh, 108
Raw Veggies with Yogurt Tzatziki, 58
Roasted Beet Salad, 47
Roasted Branzino with Lemon Potatoes, 147
Roasted Cauliflower with Quinoa and
    Mustard Dressing, 105
Roasted Eggplant Dip, 73
Roasted Red Pepper Salad, 50
Rosemary Zucchini Tomato Bake, 115
Savory Corn Muffins with Spinach and Feta, 33
Scrambled Tofu, 25
Seared Scallops, 150
Shakshuka, 27–28
Shrimp Tacos with Mango Salsa, 146
Shrimp Saganaki, 144–145
Shrimp with Zoodles, 143
Spaghetti Squash with Vegan
    Bolognese, 120–121
Spicy Shrimp Pasta Arrabbiata, 94–95
Spicy Tomato Bisque, 41–42
Strawberry Chia Jam, 172
Strawberry Ice Pops, 177
Strawberry-Peach Smoothie, 168

String Bean Casserole with Chicken, 87
Stuffed Mushrooms with Spinach and Goat
    Cheese, 66
Sweet Potato Toasts, 64
Swiss Chard Rolls with Rice in Tomato
    Sauce, 81–82
Swiss Chard Zucchini Soup, 40
Tahini Dressing, 156
Tandoori Cauliflower Curry, 114
Tangy Mustard Dressing with Apple Cider
    Vinegar, 158
Traditional Greek Salad, 45
Tri-Colored Pepper Medley with Brown
    Rice, 83–84
Tuna Burgers, 139
Tuna Lettuce Cups, 60
Tuna Salad, 140
Turkey Bolognese, 125
Turmeric Ginger Latte, 170
Unstuffed Stuffed Peppers, 127
Veal Cutlets in Green Pepper Sauce, 132
Veal Goulash, 133
Vegan Lasagna, 119
Vegan Tacos, 111
Vegetable Fried Rice, 80
Veggie Cauliflower Rice, 106
Veggie Egg Muffins, 30
Veggie Minestrone Soup, 39
Yogurt Chia Pudding, 23
GMOs (genetically modified organisms), 13
Gochugaru Sesame Seed Dressing with
    EVOO, 155
Grass-Fed Sirloin Steak with Chimichurri, 134
Greek–Style Grilled Chicken, 129
Greek–Style Quinoa Salad, 77
Greek Yogurt Marinade, 162
Green Lentil Salad with Dijon Mustard
    Dressing, 93
Green Lentil Stew, 91
Greens, 5. *See also specific*
Green Smoothie, 167
Grilled Ahi Tuna, 138
Grilled Turkey Breast Marinated in Yogurt, 124

H

Herbs, fresh, 12. *See also specific*
Homemade Chocolate Spread, 171

Homemade Granola, 18
Honey-Almond Greek Yogurt with Berries, 57

K
Kale
    Buddha Bowl, 110
    Kale and Bean Soup with Tofu, 102
    Kale Salad with Roasted Butternut
        Squash, 52
Kefir Marinade, 163

L
Leeks
    Adzuki Bean Soup, 90
    Cauliflower Chickpea Stew with Turmeric, 113
    Codfish Risotto with Saffron, 142
Lemons
    Basic EVOO and Lemon Dressing, 154
    Lemon Chicken with Capers, 128
    Lemony Asparagus Risotto, 78
    Roasted Branzino with Lemon Potatoes, 147
Chickpea Pasta with Mushrooms and
        Sage, 117–118
Lentils
    Green Lentil Salad with Dijon Mustard
        Dressing, 93
    Green Lentil Stew, 91
    Lentil Bisque, 92
Lettuce
    Butter Lettuce with Sesame Dressing, 44
    Coconut-Pineapple Smoothie, 169
    Tuna Lettuce Cups, 60

M
Mango Salsa, 160
Marinades
    Greek Yogurt Marinade, 162
    Kefir Marinade, 163
Mashed Sweet Potatoes with Spinach, 107
Mediterranean Blend, 9
Mexican-Inspired Turkey Burgers, 126
Miso Glaze, 161
Miso-Glazed Salmon, 148
Mushrooms
    Baked Cod Fillets in Mushroom Sauce, 141
    Gluten-Free Veggie Ramen Noodle
        Soup, 43

Chickpea Pasta with Mushrooms and
        Sage, 117–118
Spaghetti Squash with Vegan
        Bolognese, 120–121
Stuffed Mushrooms with Spinach and Goat
        Cheese, 66
Veggie Cauliflower Rice, 106

N
Nut-free
    Adzuki Bean Soup, 90
    Arugula Salad with Baked Acorn Squash and
        Pomegranate Seeds, 53
    Arugula Watermelon Salad, 48
    Avocado Corn Salad with Tahini Dressing, 51
    Baked Beans in Tomato Sauce, 88
    Baked Chicken Tenders, 130
    Baked Chicken Wings with Sriracha Glaze, 65
    Baked Cod Fillets in Mushroom Sauce, 141
    Baked Salmon with Parmesan
        Asparagus, 149
    Baked Sunny-Side Up Eggs with Zoodles, 29
    Baked Sweet Potato Fries with Spicy Yogurt
        Sauce, 62–63
    Baked Tuna Melts, 61
    Banana Nice-Cream, 176
    Basic EVOO and Lemon Dressing, 154
    Beans with Baby Spinach, 89
    Beef Burgers Stuffed with Feta and
        Prosciutto, 135
    Beet and Bean Hummus, 71
    Braised Cabbage with Chicken, 131
    Broccoli Pizza Crust, 67
    Buckwheat Crêpes, 173
    Buddha Bowl, 110
    Butter Lettuce with Sesame Dressing, 44
    Cauliflower Chickpea Stew with Turmeric, 113
    Chimichurri Sauce, 159
    Classic Cinnamon Oatmeal, 19
    Classic Guacamole, 59
    Coconut Oat Bran, 21
    Coconut-Pineapple Smoothie, 169
    Codfish Risotto with Saffron, 142
    Cold Bean Salad, 49
    Cold Pasta Salad, 116
    Collard Green Wraps with Vegetables and
        Tahini Dressing, 101

Creamy Broccoli Soup, 37–38
Creamy Chicken and Broccoli Pasta, 96–97
Crispy Baked Tofu, 103
Dijon Mustard Dressing, 157
Eggplant Parm, 112
Flaxseed Sesame Protein Crackers, 68
Garbanzo Bean Salad, 46
Gluten-Free Biscuits with Pumpkin and
    Sunflower Seeds, 69–70
Gluten-Free Veggie Ramen Noodle Soup, 43
Gochugaru Sesame Seed Dressing with
    EVOO, 155
Grass-Fed Sirloin Steak with Chimichurri, 134
Greek-Style Grilled Chicken, 129
Greek-Style Quinoa Salad, 77
Greek Yogurt Marinade, 162
Green Lentil Salad with Dijon Mustard
    Dressing, 93
Green Lentil Stew, 91
Green Smoothie, 167
Grilled Ahi Tuna, 138
Grilled Turkey Breast Marinated in
    Yogurt, 124
Homemade Chocolate Spread, 171
Kale and Bean Soup with Tofu, 102
Kale Salad with Roasted Butternut
    Squash, 52
Kefir Marinade, 163
Lemon Chicken with Capers, 128
Lemony Asparagus Risotto, 78
Lentil Bisque, 92
Chickpea Pasta with Mushrooms and
    Sage, 117–118
Mango Salsa, 160
Mashed Sweet Potatoes with Spinach, 107
Mexican-Inspired Turkey Burgers, 126
Miso Glaze, 161
Miso-Glazed Salmon, 148
Omelet with Spinach and Goat Cheese, 26
Overnight Chia Pudding with Berries, 24
Peanut Butter and Banana Smoothie, 166
Pea Stew with Chicken, 85–86
Protein Rice Crisps, 175
Protein Waffles with Spinach, 32
Quinoa Burrito Bowl, 109
Quinoa Tabbouleh, 108
Raw Veggies with Yogurt Tzatziki, 58

Roasted Branzino with Lemon Potatoes, 147
Roasted Cauliflower with Quinoa and
    Mustard Dressing, 105
Roasted Eggplant Dip, 73
Roasted Red Pepper Salad, 50
Rosemary Zucchini Tomato Bake, 115
Savory Corn Muffins with Spinach and
    Feta, 33
Scrambled Tofu, 25
Seared Scallops, 150
Shakshuka, 27–28
Shrimp Tacos with Mango Salsa, 146
Shrimp Saganaki, 144–145
Shrimp with Zoodles, 143
Spaghetti Squash with Vegan
    Bolognese, 120–121
Spicy Shrimp Pasta Arrabbiata, 94–95
Spicy Tomato Bisque, 41–42
Strawberry Chia Jam, 172
Strawberry Ice Pops, 177
Strawberry-Peach Smoothie, 168
String Bean Casserole with Chicken, 87
Stuffed Mushrooms with Spinach and Goat
    Cheese, 66
Sweet Potato Toasts, 64
Swiss Chard Rolls with Rice in Tomato
    Sauce, 81–82
Swiss Chard Zucchini Soup, 40
Tahini Dressing, 156
Tandoori Cauliflower Curry, 114
Tangy Mustard Dressing with Apple Cider
    Vinegar, 158
Teriyaki Tofu, 104
Traditional Greek Salad, 45
Tri-Colored Pepper Medley with Brown
    Rice, 83–84
Tuna Burgers, 139
Tuna Lettuce Cups, 60
Tuna Salad, 140
Turkey Bolognese, 125
Turmeric Ginger Latte, 170
Unstuffed Stuffed Peppers, 127
Veal Cutlets in Green Pepper Sauce, 132
Veal Goulash, 133
Vegan Lasagna, 119
Vegan Tacos, 111
Vegetable Fried Rice, 80

Nut-free *(continued)*
    Veggie Cauliflower Rice, 106
    Veggie Egg Muffins, 30
    Veggie Minestrone Soup, 39
    Yogurt Chia Pudding, 23
Nuts, 7
    Chocolate Peanut Butter Truffles, 174
    Cucumber Slices with Vegan Cream Cheese
        with Chives, 72
    Homemade Granola, 18
    Honey-Almond Greek Yogurt with Berries, 57
    Oatmeal with Baked Apples and Walnuts, 20
    Overnight Chia Pudding with Berries, 24
    Roasted Beet Salad, 47
    Walnuts, 6

O

Oat bran
    Coconut Oat Bran, 21
    Strawberry-Peach Smoothie, 168
Oatmeal with Baked Apples and Walnuts, 20
Oats, 6, 7
    Classic Cinnamon Oatmeal, 19
    Homemade Granola, 18
    Oatmeal with Baked Apples and Walnuts, 20
    Unstuffed Stuffed Peppers, 127
Olive oil, 6
    Basic EVOO and Lemon Dressing, 154
    Gochugaru Sesame Seed Dressing with
        EVOO, 155
Olives
    Cold Pasta Salad, 116
    Greek-Style Quinoa Salad, 77
    Traditional Greek Salad, 45
Omelet with Spinach and Goat Cheese, 26
Oregano
    Baked Cod Fillets in Mushroom Sauce, 141
    Chimichurri Sauce, 159
Overnight Chia and Quinoa Pudding with
    Coconut, 22
Overnight Chia Pudding with Berries, 24

P

Pantry staples, 6–10
Parsley
    Chimichurri Sauce, 159
    Cold Bean Salad, 49

    Garbanzo Bean Salad, 46
    Grass-Fed Sirloin Steak with Chimichurri, 134
    Mango Salsa, 160
    Quinoa Tabbouleh, 108
    Roasted Red Pepper Salad, 50
    Traditional Greek Salad, 45
    Tuna Salad, 140
Pasta
    Cold Pasta Salad, 116
    Creamy Chicken and Broccoli Pasta, 96–97
    Chickpea Pasta with Mushrooms and
        Sage, 117–118
    Spicy Shrimp Pasta Arrabbiata, 94–95
    Vegan Lasagna, 119
Peach-Strawberry Smoothie, 168
Peanut butter
    Chocolate Peanut Butter Truffles, 174
    Peanut Butter and Banana Smoothie, 166
Pea Stew with Chicken, 85–86
Peppers
    Cold Bean Salad, 49
    Raw Veggies with Yogurt Tzatziki, 58
    Roasted Red Pepper Salad, 50
    Scrambled Tofu, 25
    Shakshuka, 27–28
    Tri-Colored Pepper Medley with Brown
        Rice, 83–84
    Unstuffed Stuffed Peppers, 127
    Veal Cutlets in Green Pepper Sauce, 132
    Veggie Egg Muffins, 30
Pesticides, 12–13
Pineapple-Coconut Smoothie, 169
Pizza Crust, Broccoli, 67
Pomegranate Seeds, Arugula Salad with Baked
    Acorn Squash and, 53
Potatoes. *See also* Sweet potatoes
    Braised Cabbage with Chicken, 131
    Pea Stew with Chicken, 85–86
    Roasted Branzino with Lemon Potatoes, 147
    Rosemary Zucchini Tomato Bake, 115
    Swiss Chard Rolls with Rice in Tomato
        Sauce, 81–82
Produce selection, 4
Prosciutto and Feta, Beef Burgers Stuffed
    with, 135
Protein Rice Crisps, 175
Protein Waffles with Spinach, 32

Pumpkin seeds, 6
    Arugula Salad with Baked Acorn Squash and
        Pomegranate Seeds, 53
    Gluten-Free Biscuits with Pumpkin and
        Sunflower Seeds, 69–70
    Kale Salad with Roasted Butternut
        Squash, 52
    Protein Rice Crisps, 175

Q
Quinoa, 6
    Greek-Style Quinoa Salad, 77
    Overnight Chia and Quinoa Pudding with
        Coconut, 22
    Quinoa Burrito Bowl, 109
    Quinoa Tabbouleh, 108
    Roasted Cauliflower with Quinoa and
        Mustard Dressing, 105

R
Raw Veggies with Yogurt Tzatziki, 58
Recipes, about, 14
Refrigerator staples, 10–11
Rice
    Codfish Risotto with Saffron, 142
    Lemony Asparagus Risotto, 78
    Protein Rice Crisps, 175
    Swiss Chard Rolls with Rice in Tomato
        Sauce, 81–82
    Tri-Colored Pepper Medley with Brown
        Rice, 83–84
    Vegetable Fried Rice, 80
Roasted Beet Salad, 47
Roasted Branzino with Lemon Potatoes, 147
Roasted Cauliflower with Quinoa and Mustard
    Dressing, 105
Roasted Eggplant Dip, 73
Roasted Red Pepper Salad, 50
Rosemary Zucchini Tomato Bake, 115

S
Saffron, Codfish Risotto with, 142
Sage, Chickpea Pasta with Mushrooms
    and, 117–118
Salads. See also Bowls; Dressings
    Arugula Salad with Baked Acorn Squash and
        Pomegranate Seeds, 53

Arugula Watermelon Salad, 48
Avocado Corn Salad with Tahini Dressing, 51
Butter Lettuce with Sesame Dressing, 44
Cold Bean Salad, 49
Cold Pasta Salad, 116
Garbanzo Bean Salad, 46
Greek-Style Quinoa Salad, 77
Green Lentil Salad with Dijon Mustard
    Dressing, 93
Kale Salad with Roasted Butternut
    Squash, 52
Quinoa Tabbouleh, 108
Roasted Beet Salad, 47
Roasted Red Pepper Salad, 50
Traditional Greek Salad, 45
Tuna Lettuce Cups, 60
Tuna Salad, 140
Salmon, 6
    Baked Salmon with Parmesan
        Asparagus, 149
    Miso-Glazed Salmon, 148
Sandwiches and wraps. See also
        Burgers; Tacos
    Baked Tuna Melts, 61
    Collard Green Wraps with Vegetables and
        Tahini Dressing, 101
    Tuna Salad, 140
Sauces. See also Marinades
    Chimichurri Sauce, 159
    Mango Salsa, 160
    Miso Glaze, 161
    Turkey Bolognese, 125
Savory Corn Muffins with Spinach and Feta, 33
Scrambled Tofu, 25
Seared Scallops, 150
Seasonal eating, 4
Seasonings, 7–9
Sesame seeds
    Baked Salmon with Parmesan
        Asparagus, 149
    Flaxseed Sesame Protein Crackers, 68
    Gochugaru Sesame Seed Dressing with
        EVOO, 155
Shakshuka, 27–28
Shrimp
    Shrimp Tacos with Mango Salsa, 146
    Shrimp Saganaki, 144–145

Shrimp (*continued*)
    Shrimp with Zoodles, 143
    Spicy Shrimp Pasta Arrabbiata, 94–95
Smoothies
    Coconut-Pineapple Smoothie, 169
    Green Smoothie, 167
    Peanut Butter and Banana Smoothie, 166
    Strawberry-Peach Smoothie, 168
Snacks
    Baked Chicken Wings with Sriracha
        Glaze, 65
    Baked Sweet Potato Fries with Spicy Yogurt
        Sauce, 62–63
    Beet and Bean Hummus, 71
    Classic Guacamole, 59
    Cucumber Slices with Vegan Cream Cheese
        and Chives, 72
    Flaxseed Sesame Protein Crackers, 68
    Honey-Almond Greek Yogurt with Berries, 57
    Raw Veggies with Yogurt Tzatziki, 58
    Roasted Eggplant Dip, 73
    Stuffed Mushrooms with Spinach and Goat
        Cheese, 66
    Sweet Potato Toasts, 64
Soups. *See also* Stews
    Adzuki Bean Soup, 90
    Creamy Broccoli Soup, 37–38
    Gluten-Free Veggie Ramen Noodle Soup, 43
    Kale and Bean Soup with Tofu, 102
    Lentil Bisque, 92
    Spicy Tomato Bisque, 41–42
    Swiss Chard Zucchini Soup, 40
    Veggie Minestrone Soup, 39
Soy-free
    Adzuki Bean Soup, 90
    American Protein Pancakes, 31
    Arugula Salad with Baked Acorn Squash and
        Pomegranate Seeds, 53
    Arugula Watermelon Salad, 48
    Avocado Corn Salad with Tahini Dressing, 51
    Baked Beans in Tomato Sauce, 88
    Baked Chicken Tenders, 130
    Baked Chicken Wings with Sriracha Glaze, 65
    Baked Cod Fillets in Mushroom Sauce, 141
    Baked Salmon with Parmesan
        Asparagus, 149
    Baked Sunny-Side Up Eggs with Zoodles, 29

Baked Sweet Potato Fries with Spicy Yogurt
    Sauce, 62–63
Baked Tuna Melts, 61
Banana Nice-Cream, 176
Basic EVOO and Lemon Dressing, 154
Beans with Baby Spinach, 89
Beef Burgers Stuffed with Feta and
    Prosciutto, 135
Beet and Bean Hummus, 71
Braised Cabbage with Chicken, 131
Broccoli Pizza Crust, 67
Buckwheat Crêpes, 173
Buddha Bowl, 110
Butter Lettuce with Sesame Dressing, 44
Cauliflower Chickpea Stew with Turmeric, 113
Chimichurri Sauce, 159
Chocolate Peanut Butter Truffles, 174
Classic Cinnamon Oatmeal, 19
Classic Guacamole, 59
Coconut Oat Bran, 21
Coconut-Pineapple Smoothie, 169
Codfish Risotto with Saffron, 142
Cold Bean Salad, 49
Cold Pasta Salad, 116
Collard Green Wraps with Vegetables and
    Tahini Dressing, 101
Creamy Broccoli Soup, 37–38
Creamy Chicken and Broccoli Pasta, 96–97
Crispy Baked Tofu, 103
Cucumber Slices with Vegan Cream Cheese
    and Chives, 72
Dijon Mustard Dressing, 157
Eggplant Parm, 112
Flaxseed Sesame Protein Crackers, 68
Garbanzo Bean Salad, 46
Gluten-Free Biscuits with Pumpkin and
    Sunflower Seeds, 69–70
Gluten-Free Veggie Ramen Noodle Soup, 43
Gochugaru Sesame Seed Dressing with
    EVOO, 155
Grass-Fed Sirloin Steak with Chimichurri, 134
Greek–Style Grilled Chicken, 129
Greek–Style Quinoa Salad, 77
Greek Yogurt Marinade, 162
Green Lentil Salad with Dijon Mustard
    Dressing, 93
Green Lentil Stew, 91

Green Smoothie, 167
Grilled Turkey Breast Marinated in
    Yogurt, 124
Homemade Chocolate Spread, 171
Homemade Granola, 18
Honey-Almond Greek Yogurt with Berries, 57
Kale Salad with Roasted Butternut
    Squash, 52
Kefir Marinade, 163
Lemon Chicken with Capers, 128
Lemony Asparagus Risotto, 78
Lentil Bisque, 92
Chickpea Pasta with Mushrooms and
    Sage, 117–118
Mango Salsa, 160
Mashed Sweet Potatoes with Spinach, 107
Mexican-Inspired Turkey Burgers, 126
Oatmeal with Baked Apples and Walnuts, 20
Omelet with Spinach and Goat Cheese, 26
Overnight Chia and Quinoa Pudding with
    Coconut, 22
Overnight Chia Pudding with Berries, 24
Peanut Butter and Banana Smoothie, 166
Pea Stew with Chicken, 85–86
Protein Rice Crisps, 175
Protein Waffles with Spinach, 32
Quinoa Burrito Bowl, 109
Quinoa Tabbouleh, 108
Raw Veggies with Yogurt Tzatziki, 58
Roasted Beet Salad, 47
Roasted Branzino with Lemon Potatoes, 147
Roasted Cauliflower with Quinoa and
    Mustard Dressing, 105
Roasted Eggplant Dip, 73
Roasted Red Pepper Salad, 50
Rosemary Zucchini Tomato Bake, 115
Savory Corn Muffins with Spinach and
    Feta, 33
Seared Scallops, 150
Shakshuka, 27–28
Shrimp Tacos with Mango Salsa, 146
Shrimp Saganaki, 144–145
Shrimp with Zoodles, 143
Spicy Shrimp Pasta Arrabbiata, 94–95
Spicy Tomato Bisque, 41–42
Strawberry Chia Jam, 172
Strawberry Ice Pops, 177

Strawberry-Peach Smoothie, 168
String Bean Casserole with Chicken, 87
Stuffed Mushrooms with Spinach and Goat
    Cheese, 66
Sweet Potato Toasts, 64
Swiss Chard Rolls with Rice in Tomato
    Sauce, 81–82
Swiss Chard Zucchini Soup, 40
Tahini Dressing, 156
Tandoori Cauliflower Curry, 114
Tangy Mustard Dressing with Apple Cider
    Vinegar, 158
Traditional Greek Salad, 45
Tri-Colored Pepper Medley with Brown
    Rice, 83–84
Tuna Burgers, 139
Tuna Lettuce Cups, 60
Tuna Salad, 140
Turkey Bolognese, 125
Turmeric Ginger Latte, 170
Unstuffed Stuffed Peppers, 127
Veal Cutlets in Green Pepper Sauce, 132
Veal Goulash, 133
Vegan Lasagna, 119
Vegan Tacos, 111
Vegetable Fried Rice, 80
Veggie Egg Muffins, 30
Veggie Minestrone Soup, 39
Yogurt Chia Pudding, 23
Spaghetti Squash with Vegan
    Bolognese, 120–121
Spices, 7–9
Spicy Shrimp Pasta Arrabbiata, 94–95
Spicy Tomato Bisque, 41–42
Spinach
    Beans with Baby Spinach, 89
    Green Smoothie, 167
    Mashed Sweet Potatoes with Spinach, 107
    Omelet with Spinach and Goat Cheese, 26
    Peanut Butter and Banana Smoothie, 166
    Protein Waffles with Spinach, 32
    Savory Corn Muffins with Spinach and
        Feta, 33
    Stuffed Mushrooms with Spinach and Goat
        Cheese, 66
    Tuna Burgers, 139
    Vegan Lasagna, 119

Squash. *See also* Zucchini
    Arugula Salad with Baked Acorn Squash and
        Pomegranate Seeds, 53
    Kale Salad with Roasted Butternut
        Squash, 52
    Spaghetti Squash with Vegan
        Bolognese, 120–121
Sriracha
    Baked Chicken Wings with Sriracha
        Glaze, 65
    Baked Sweet Potato Fries with Spicy Yogurt
        Sauce, 62–63
Stews
    Cauliflower Chickpea Stew with Turmeric, 113
    Green Lentil Stew, 91
    Pea Stew with Chicken, 85–86
    Veal Goulash, 133
Strawberry Chia Jam, 172
Strawberry Ice Pops, 177
Strawberry-Peach Smoothie, 168
String Bean Casserole with Chicken, 87
Stuffed Mushrooms with Spinach and Goat
    Cheese, 66
Sunflower seeds
    Gluten-Free Biscuits with Pumpkin and
        Sunflower Seeds, 69–70
Superfoods, 5–6
Sweet potatoes
    Baked Sweet Potato Fries with Spicy Yogurt
        Sauce, 62–63
    Collard Green Wraps with Vegetables and
        Tahini Dressing, 101
    Mashed Sweet Potatoes with Spinach, 107
    Sweet Potato Toasts, 64
    Swiss Chard Zucchini Soup, 40
Swiss Chard Rolls with Rice in Tomato
    Sauce, 81–82
Swiss Chard Zucchini Soup, 40

T

Tacos
    Shrimp Tacos with Mango Salsa, 146
    Vegan Tacos, 111
Taco Seasoning, 9
Tahini
    Beet and Bean Hummus, 71
    Chocolate Peanut Butter Truffles, 174
    Collard Green Wraps with Vegetables and
        Tahini Dressing, 101
    Homemade Chocolate Spread, 171
    Roasted Eggplant Dip, 73
    Tahini Dressing, 156
Tandoori Cauliflower Curry, 114
Tangy Mustard Dressing with Apple Cider
    Vinegar, 158
Teriyaki Tofu, 104
Tofu
    Crispy Baked Tofu, 103
    Kale and Bean Soup with Tofu, 102
    Scrambled Tofu, 25
    Teriyaki Tofu, 104
    Vegan Lasagna, 119
    Vegan Tacos, 111
Tomatoes
    Baked Beans in Tomato Sauce, 88
    Baked Cod Fillets in Mushroom
        Sauce, 141
    Beans with Baby Spinach, 89
    Classic Guacamole, 59
    Garbanzo Bean Salad, 46
    Greek-Style Quinoa Salad, 77
    Green Lentil Salad with Dijon Mustard
        Dressing, 93
    Rosemary Zucchini Tomato Bake, 115
    Shakshuka, 27–28
    Shrimp Saganaki, 144–145
    Spaghetti Squash with Vegan
        Bolognese, 120–121
    Spicy Shrimp Pasta Arrabbiata, 94–95
    Spicy Tomato Bisque, 41–42
    Traditional Greek Salad, 45
    Tri-Colored Pepper Medley with Brown
        Rice, 83–84
    Veggie Minestrone Soup, 39
Toxins, 12–13
Traditional Greek Salad, 45
Tri-Colored Pepper Medley with Brown
    Rice, 83–84
Tuna
    Baked Tuna Melts, 61
    Grilled Ahi Tuna, 138
    Tuna Burgers, 139
    Tuna Lettuce Cups, 60
    Tuna Salad, 140

Turkey
    Grilled Turkey Breast Marinated in
        Yogurt, 124
    Mexican-Inspired Turkey Burgers, 126
    Turkey Bolognese, 125
    Unstuffed Stuffed Peppers, 127
Turmeric, 6
Turmeric Ginger Latte, 170

U
Unstuffed Stuffed Peppers, 127

V
Veal Cutlets in Green Pepper Sauce, 132
Veal Goulash, 133
Vegan
    Adzuki Bean Soup, 90
    Arugula Salad with Baked Acorn Squash and
        Pomegranate Seeds, 53
    Avocado Corn Salad with Tahini Dressing, 51
    Baked Beans in Tomato Sauce, 88
    Baked Sweet Potato Fries with Spicy Yogurt
        Sauce, 62–63
    Banana Nice-Cream, 176
    Basic EVOO and Lemon Dressing, 154
    Beet and Bean Hummus, 71
    Broccoli Pizza Crust, 67
    Buddha Bowl, 110
    Butter Lettuce with Sesame Dressing, 44
    Cauliflower Chickpea Stew with
        Turmeric, 113
    Chocolate Peanut Butter Truffles, 174
    Classic Cinnamon Oatmeal, 19
    Classic Guacamole, 59
    Coconut Oat Bran, 21
    Coconut-Pineapple Smoothie, 169
    Cold Bean Salad, 49
    Cold Pasta Salad, 116
    Collard Green Wraps with Vegetables and
        Tahini Dressing, 101
    Crispy Baked Tofu, 103
    Cucumber Slices with Vegan Cream Cheese
        and Chives, 72
    Dijon Mustard Dressing, 157
    Eggplant Parm, 112
    Flaxseed Sesame Protein Crackers, 68
    Garbanzo Bean Salad, 46

Gluten-Free Biscuits with Pumpkin and
    Sunflower Seeds, 69–70
Gluten-Free Veggie Ramen Noodle Soup, 43
Greek-Style Quinoa Salad, 77
Green Lentil Salad with Dijon Mustard
    Dressing, 93
Green Lentil Stew, 91
Green Smoothie, 167
Homemade Chocolate Spread, 171
Homemade Granola, 18
Kale and Bean Soup with Tofu, 102
Kale Salad with Roasted Butternut
    Squash, 52
Chickpea Pasta with Mushrooms and
    Sage, 117–118
Mashed Sweet Potatoes with Spinach, 107
Oatmeal with Baked Apples and Walnuts, 20
Overnight Chia and Quinoa Pudding with
    Coconut, 22
Peanut Butter and Banana Smoothie, 166
Protein Rice Crisps, 175
Quinoa Burrito Bowl, 109
Quinoa Tabbouleh, 108
Roasted Cauliflower with Quinoa and
    Mustard Dressing, 105
Roasted Eggplant Dip, 73
Roasted Red Pepper Salad, 50
Rosemary Zucchini Tomato Bake, 115
Scrambled Tofu, 25
Spaghetti Squash with Vegan
    Bolognese, 120–121
Spicy Tomato Bisque, 41–42
Strawberry Chia Jam, 172
Strawberry Ice Pops, 177
Strawberry-Peach Smoothie, 168
Sweet Potato Toasts, 64
Swiss Chard Rolls with Rice in Tomato
    Sauce, 81–82
Swiss Chard Zucchini Soup, 40
Tahini Dressing, 156
Tandoori Cauliflower Curry, 114
Teriyaki Tofu, 104
Turmeric Ginger Latte, 170
Vegan Lasagna, 119
Vegan Tacos, 111
Veggie Cauliflower Rice, 106
Veggie Minestrone Soup, 39

Vegetable Fried Rice, 80
Vegetables, 4, 10–13. *See also specific*
Vegetarian. *See also* Vegan
　American Protein Pancakes, 31
　Arugula Watermelon Salad, 48
　Baked Sunny-Side Up Eggs with Zoodles, 29
　Basic EVOO and Lemon Dressing, 154
　Buckwheat Crêpes, 173
　Creamy Broccoli Soup, 37–38
　Dijon Mustard Dressing, 157
　Gochugaru Sesame Seed Dressing with
　　EVOO, 155
　Greek Yogurt Marinade, 162
　Honey-Almond Greek Yogurt with
　　Berries, 57
　Kefir Marinade, 163
　Lemony Asparagus Risotto, 78
　Lentil Bisque, 92
　Miso Glaze, 161
　Omelet with Spinach and Goat Cheese, 26
　Overnight Chia Pudding with Berries, 24
　Protein Waffles with Spinach, 32
　Raw Veggies with Yogurt Tzatziki, 58
　Roasted Beet Salad, 47
　Savory Corn Muffins with Spinach and
　　Feta, 33
　Shakshuka, 27–28
　Swiss Chard Rolls with Rice in Tomato
　　Sauce, 81–82
　Tahini Dressing, 156
　Tangy Mustard Dressing with Apple Cider
　　Vinegar, 158
　Traditional Greek Salad, 45
　Vegetable Fried Rice, 80

Veggie Egg Muffins, 30
Yogurt Chia Pudding, 23
Veggie Cauliflower Rice, 106
Veggie Egg Muffins, 30
Veggie Minestrone Soup, 39

W
Watermelon Arugula Salad, 48

Y
Yogurt
　Baked Sweet Potato Fries with Spicy Yogurt
　　Sauce, 62–63
　Greek Yogurt Marinade, 162
　Grilled Turkey Breast Marinated in
　　Yogurt, 124
　Honey-Almond Greek Yogurt with Berries, 57
　Overnight Chia Pudding with Berries, 24
　Raw Veggies with Yogurt Tzatziki, 58
　Savory Corn Muffins with Spinach and
　　Feta, 33
　String Bean Casserole with Chicken, 87
　Yogurt Chia Pudding, 23

Z
Zucchini
　Baked Sunny-Side Up Eggs with Zoodles, 29
　Gluten-Free Veggie Ramen Noodle Soup, 43
　Rosemary Zucchini Tomato Bake, 115
　Shrimp with Zoodles, 143
　Swiss Chard Zucchini Soup, 40
　Tandoori Cauliflower Curry, 114
　Veggie Egg Muffins, 30
　Veggie Minestrone Soup, 39

ACKNOWLEDGMENTS

This cookbook is a dream come true for me, but it would not be possible without my family, friends, my Instagram community, the Institute for Integrative Nutrition (IIN) and, of course, my editors at Callisto Media.

To my husband, my rock. I would not be the woman I am today without your loving, endless support. Thank you for loving my cooking for so many years now. Cooking for you and our kids makes me happy beyond words. I'm grateful for our beautiful life we have created together. My Mia and Luka, one day you will understand why Mommy made you eat vegetables and said no to chips and fast food restaurants. Your singing, dancing, and silliness bring joy to my life every day.

To my dad, who raised me to become the strong woman that I am today. I'm grateful for the homemade meals, daily bike rides along the Danube River, and amazing summers spent in our mountain house. To my mom, who always said "You can and you will" and supported me beyond limits. You believed in me when I did not and encouraged me always to trust my intuition and follow my dreams. To my little brother, who is always there. Thank you for your unselfish love for me and my kids. I hope that Mia, Luka, and Lara will have a bond like we do.

My friends, whom I love dearly. Barbecue parties, birthday parties, New Year's Eve celebrations, and vacations together are always in my heart.

To my Instagram community, this book is inspired by all of you amazing people who have been with me since the beginning. Your comments, your own creations of my recipes, and your messages mean the world to me. I am inspired by you and appreciate you every day.

I'm thankful for the wonderful nutrition program at IIN that was the core of a new chapter in my life. This school played a major role in my health transformation and my career as a health coach. Thank you for opening so many doors for me. Being part of this school and community taught me many life lessons that I will cherish forever.

Callisto Media team, I am so lucky you found me. Thank you for trusting me with this cookbook and giving me this opportunity. Thank you for leading me and making the book-writing process seamless.

ABOUT THE AUTHOR

Having transformed her own life, **Snezana Paucinac** was determined to help others around her. In her health coaching career, she was fortunate enough to meet many incredible people and lead them toward becoming their healthiest, best version of themselves. Her love for nutrition and healthy living led Snezana to create a successful social media platform where she shares her recipes, nutritious meal ideas, and healthy living tips.

Snezana currently lives in Belgrade, Serbia, where she grew up, with her two kids, Mia and Luka, her husband, Boris, and their bulldog pup, Toby. Spending time with her family, traveling, and creating memories are things Snezana cherishes every day.

With this cookbook, Snezana hopes to inspire more people to see the beauty in cooking and homemade meals, and to realize that being healthy is not a chore, but rather a beautiful lifestyle.